Bad News
Religion

Bad News

Religion

The Virus that Attacks God's Grace

Greg Albrecht

Published in Nashville, Tennessee by World Publishing.
www.worldpublishing.com

ISBN 0-529-11954-4

Printed in the United States of America

1 2 3 4 5 — 08 07 06 05 04

Contents

Acknowledgments

BAD NEWS RELIGION is dedicated to religious refugees everywhere. When I explain to new acquaintances that I minister to refugees and prisoners who are burned out with religion, many immediately identify and start to tell me their story. On the other hand, others react as if I had just confessed to being a serial murderer. Such people attempt to lecture me (a staple of legalism, the good old fashioned scrub-brush scolding), warning me that I am going too far with this grace thing. Their real concern is that grace might throw their methodical, regulated world into upheaval. They have every right to be concerned. It will.

I thank my wife Karen, who knew me as a slave to religious legalism, and put up with me as God helped me to leave the illusion of safety offered by legalism in order to accept freedom in Christ (Galatians 5:1). As this book is published, we will celebrate, God willing, our 35th anniversary of marriage. Even more importantly, we thank God that we are well into our second decade of living by faith alone, grace alone, and Christ alone. Thank you, Karen, for your love and support.

My special thanks to "fellow refugees" Monte Wolverton, Laura Urista, Phylllis Duke, and Marv Wegner. They each have their own past encounters with *Bad News Religion*. Monte has helped to edit and revise this manuscript through many hours of discussion. Laura, Phyllis, and Marv have provided invaluable skills in pre-print production. Marv also contributed the initial graphic ideas for our cover design.

Many thanks to Thomas Nelson and World Publishing. I am honored that someone with the wisdom and experience of Sam Moore encouraged me to share this message. Ted Squires and Randy Elliott were no doubt visionaries in seeing something of value in the initial manuscript, and Frank Couch of World Publishing has been a helpful and gracious editor in coaxing the final version out of me—the one you hold in your hands.

To all religious refugees everywhere—don't give up on God because of *Bad News Religion!* He wants you to experience his grace and accept the freedom he gives you in Christ.

Bad News
Religion

1

From There to Eternity

"I went looking for spirit and found alcohol; I went looking for soul, and I bought some style; I wanted to meet God, but they sold me religion."

—U-2's Bono,
quoted in *Walk On: The Spiritual Journey of U-2,*
Steve Stokman

LIFE OFTEN HAPPENS TO US while we are doing something else. It happens while we are busy working, raising a family, paying the bills, and getting old. Then one day we stop to catch our breath, and we start asking some questions. Why am I in such a big rush to get where I am going? And, for that matter, where exactly am I going? Why do I think, believe and behave the way I do? Why was I born? Is there really any purpose in my life? A movie and song from my youth pleads, *What's It All About, Alfie?* One of the important Alfies of my life was a man named Alexander. Alexander arrived in the port of Galveston, Texas in the early years of the 20th century. He was a teenager, running away from religious hatred and war. Alex came to America as a refugee, and he didn't want anything to do with what he had left behind. He saw the past as better forgotten than remembered.

Alex found his way north, through Texas and Oklahoma, eventually settling down in Herington, Kansas. He married and with his wife Martha had twelve children. Alex and Martha were proud that their children and grandchildren were citizens, by birth, of a new and free country. One of their children was named Alice—Alice was my mother.

Along with most of her siblings my mother spent many of her adult years trying to discover her heritage. She hungered to know more about who she was. She knew that her father had come from either Germany or Russia, or perhaps both. That's all my Grandpa Alex would volunteer. The old country was not something he wanted to talk about. He offered no stories about the past, leaving his children with no continuity or context. The old country was bad news, and he had come to America dreaming of a fresh chance, a new start.

The unresolved mystery caused intense family speculation. Were our ancestors a part of a large colony of Germans who had once lived in Russia? Did the past Alex left behind include an ethnic and religious purge that he survived? Or, was the secret even more bizarre —was it possible that Alex had suffered because he had Jewish blood, a past that he concealed because he didn't want his family to experience any of the suffering he had seen? Speculations abounded, but the truth was never shared.

One thing was clear. Grandpa Alex had little time for what he knew of religion. He believed in God, but distrusted organizations and incorporated churches that claimed to speak for and represent God. It took almost five decades of my life to discover how much of his blood flows in my veins.

I still don't know much about Alexander's past. Perhaps I never will. My maternal grandmother and both paternal grandparents felt the same way about the old country. They arrived in the United States early in the 20th century and wanted no part of the past. This was a new country, a new life. They lived in the present, working and sacrificing for the future.

I never could completely understand how my grandparents felt about the old country. The entire family wanted to know about our roots. We wanted to be connected with our story, no matter how brutal, gruesome or ugly that story might be. My grandparents had all died, as indeed had both my parents, when I finally started to understand why they wanted to leave the old country behind.

From Luther to a Cult

One day almost 70 years after my grandfather's arrival in Galveston, Texas, his daughter (and my mother) poured out her heart to me. She felt that she had unwittingly been trapped by a religious disaster with some similarities to the religious strife that had caused her father to leave the old country behind. She was profoundly sorry that she had introduced me to and involved me in what later became known as Armstrongism—the legalistic and cultic teachings of Herbert W. Armstrong. It was the early 1980s, and I was very much a true blue believer in Armstrongism.

At the time my mother was tearfully confiding in me, I was the Dean of Students of Ambassador College in Pasadena, California. I taught classes and served as the pastor of 500 college students, many of whom eventually found their way into career service within the Armstrong empire. I was an ordained minister of the Worldwide Church of God, founded by Armstrong over 40 years before. As a minister and faculty member I administered restrictive and rigorous rules and policies for students, some of which I did not adhere to in my own life. That irony, indeed that hypocrisy, would hit me hard in a few more years.

My mother had become disenchanted with a church for which

she had sacrificed. For almost three decades my mother and my stepfather had given the church much of their time and their money—and she was burned out. My mother was no scholar, but she had been reading and researching. She had a copy of Eric Hofer's *The True Believer* in her trembling hands. "Greg," she said, her eyes moist with tears, "we are in a cult. I am sorry that I got you into this whole mess. I wish we had just stayed in the Lutheran church."

She then rehearsed a story I had heard so many times as a young boy—the painful story of the death and funeral of my father, Elmer Otto Albrecht. Elmer was a Kansas farm boy who fell in love with and married Alice, a teenager who lived in the town of Herington. Elmer was my mother's one true love, the father I never knew. Returning to Kansas following service in the Navy during WW II, my father purchased a dairy with another man. Fifteen months after I was born my father was electrocuted as he cleaned the dairy following his day at work. My mother canonized my father in my eyes, making this larger-than-life hero into a saint, a hard working man loved by one and all, and especially by my mother.

> **I spent the next 35 years of my life up to my neck in this specific religious swamp, in what I have now come to see, by God's grace, as *40 Miles of Bad Road*.**

His death was a tragedy in the little town of Herington. It was a story my mother told me over and over again. She wanted me to know as much as I could about the father I never knew. She felt a void, not knowing as much as she would have liked about her own past, and didn't want me to share the same fate. Her hands gripping *The True Believer* as if it were a sacred book, my mother reminded me that I had been baptized in the Lutheran church, in whose cemetery my father was buried. And she pleaded with me to read Hofer's book, and to consider leaving what she was now calling the cult.

I was in my early 30's, married with two children in school, and on my way up in the Armstrong empire. *I was a true believer,* and although I knew that many people "in the world" thought Armstrongism was a cult, I knew better. I also knew better than my mother, so I comforted her and assured her that we were in the true church—the "one and only true church."

There were lots of rules in the one true church of Armstrongism. No pork or shellfish. No Christmas or Easter. No birthdays. No make up or cosmetics for women. No voting or service on a jury. No involvement in politics. No "worldly" friends (as a young man I found ways to get around this one).

No participation or involvement in work or sports on Friday night or Saturday. During these 24 hours of "holy time" virtually nothing could be done, except go to church. No shopping. No television. No secular reading. No cooking. In early Armstrongism some people didn't even make their beds on Saturday, a restriction that would have been fine with the young Greg Albrecht—but my Germanic mother never did buy into that one.

Three tithes were demanded—one directly to the church, one to save so that families could observe the Armstrong version of the Hebrew holy day calendar, and a third ten percent to give to the church every third year so that the church could provide for its poor. My mother and stepfather never owned a house. They never felt that they could maintain the payments in addition to their financial support of Armstrongism. They rented houses, and in their later years they lived in an apartment.

As a young man I was taught that I was a special and unique kind of Christian. I was a part of the only true Christian church. All other

Christians were "falsely so-called" Christians. But my Lutheran family back in Kansas, and the few childhood friends I managed to make that were outside of Armstrongism were confused. It seemed to them that much of what I did and did not do conformed to Judaism. So, if it walks like a duck and talks like a duck, it must be a duck. Looking back, I now conclude that the Armstrongism I believed in was a cult based upon modified Judaism, all in the name of Jesus Christ.

And now, having grown up in Armstrongism, and achieved some standing within the hierarchy, I was sitting with my mother in her apartment, watching her shaking hands and resolute expression, hearing her tell me that all of it was just another cult. My mind drifted back almost 30 years to another apartment where it all started—this one in Longview, Texas.

THE FIRST STEPS ON *40 MILES OF BAD ROAD*

After my father died my mother and I traveled, living with relatives, as she searched for the solution to the challenges of being what is now called a single parent. At the time society identified her as a young widow. We lived in Kansas, Colorado, Texas, and California— always with family, always with uncles who would provide a positive male role model for me.

One of those role models was Walt Molpus, who worked for LeTourneu heavy equipment in Longview, Texas. Walt was married to one of my mother's older sisters, Bernice. My uncle Walt and aunt Bernice were wonderful to us, providing us with help and family support during times that must have been desperately lonely for my mother. My mother was looking for a father for me, but more than that she was looking for context and spiritual identity. She was what we now call a seeker.

Walt introduced my mother to a coworker at LeTourneu, Lewis

Greenwood, a man who would later become my stepfather. My mother's budding relationship with Lewis caused her to get an apartment in Longview, where I attended the first grade.

Like my father, Lewis Greenwood was a veteran of the Navy, and during his WW II service he had heard Herbert W. Armstrong on the radio. As so many others who heard these broadcasts, Lewis was ill equipped to deal with Armstrong's compelling, bombastic style coupled with his unbiblical truth claims. Lewis grew up in Duncan, Oklahoma, as a Baptist—but the message of Armstrongism was appealing to him because he was, at that time, a nominal Christian at best. When my mother married Lewis we all took a long detour from Christianity into the swamps of cultic religion. Armstrongism proved to be a rigid and remote outpost in the badlands of religion that gave me some never-to-be-forgotten experiences in legalism, all in the name of Christianity and the Bible.

After their wedding Alice and Lewis honeymooned in Galveston—the port where her father had arrived in America for a new life almost 40 years before. They quickly became members of Herbert Armstrong's church, then called the Radio Church of God. We moved to south Texas to be closer to another special family that had also "adopted" my mother and me. My mother's oldest sister Esther and her husband Alvin had four children, cousins who shared the endless adventures available on their farm with me. They even gave me the high honor of helping them chop and pick cotton.

Although I was only in second grade, I was very much aware of the disapproval of Armstrongism on the part of my extended family. My surrogate fathers Alvin and Walt were always tactful about my mother and stepfather's strange new beliefs, but even as a seven-year-old boy I could sense displeasure and even sadness. Alienation escalated as my mother and stepfather hurtled headlong into religious fanaticism—with me firmly in tow.

I spent the next 35 years of my life up to my neck in this specific religious swamp, in what I have now come to see, by God's grace, as *40 Miles of Bad Road* (with apologies to Duane Eddy, who back in the day had a hit record by the same name). I attended second and third grade in Rosenberg, Texas, and then we moved to Pasadena, California, to be at the world headquarters of Armstrongism and his college, Ambassador College. I grew up in southern California receiving the best indoctrination Armstrongism could give, in both elementary and secondary school as well as Ambassador College.

Assigned as a student to Armstrong's college campus in England, I met and later married my wife Karen, whose family has its own story of becoming seduced by Armstrongism. Our wedding ceremony, at our request, was personally officiated by Herbert W. Armstrong. It wasn't until many years later that I realized and reflected about the radically different experience of another American our age who was also a student in England at the same time. The university that future President of the United States Bill Clinton attended was less than 100 miles away from the strict and severe campus experience my wife and I endured, but those 100 miles were light years away. Armstrongism was and is an alternative reality, in the language of *Star Wars*, "a galaxy far, far away." My wife and I, along with a number of other fellow students at Armstrong's English campus, were marching down *40 Miles of Bad Road.*

After graduation we were assigned and enlisted into "the work" of Armstrongism. Our service, much like that of the military, was assigned, without regard for our preference. We remained in England, partially because, as I discovered later, several senior leaders in the English branch of the movement weren't finished with me yet. They were, in their own way, fond of us. In their wrong-headed and hardheaded legalistic and cultic thinking, they felt that Karen and I needed "further training"—boot camp would have been a more accurate description.

Once it was decided we had paid our dues, we were transferred back to the world headquarters in California, to the much-envied position of faculty member at Ambassador College. As a young couple with two pre-school age children we were felt to be good role models to help train others who would follow in our footsteps, becoming soldiers in the cause.

The legalistic requirements of Armstrongism appeared on the surface to have much in common with American Protestant fundamentalism, yet underneath there were important differences: a devotion to Old Covenant Jewish requirements, eclectic teachings about the nature of God, the myth of British Israelism, and a host of other fables and heretical notions. A potent strain of the holiness movement influenced Herbert Armstrong, the idea that righteousness could be obtained by virtue of personal effort and achievement. For all of its deviation from historical Christianity, the most toxic of all of the teachings of Armstrongism is legalism. One can never be good enough in Armstrongism—there is always another rule to obey, another task to accomplish, more character to build, and another personal problem or secret sin to overcome. Never good enough—it's the theme song of *Bad News Religion*.

THE TRUE BELIEVER

By the early 1980's my wife and I had been judged to be worthy of continued advancement in the hierarchy. I had moved up the ranks by the time my mother tearfully confronted me with the truth that we were in a cult and apologized for her role in placing her grandchildren and me in this "mess." Each advancement solidified my commitment and took me deeper into the swamps of *Bad News*

Religion, with me becoming a more naïve true believer. *Bad News Religion* is based on the conviction that if we do more and try harder we will be able to manipulate and obligate God into accepting our good deeds as at least partial payment for our salvation.

Exclusive and elitist teachings and practices characterized my life as I moved up the ladder from a foot soldier to a leader in a religion that called itself Christian. I did not realize at the time that I was a narrow, judgmental, hypercritical, faultfinding slave of *Bad News Religion.* But my Lord and Savior introduced me to grace, and grace would eventually turn my world upside down.

Within a few years after I rejected my mother's plea to leave the cult of Armstrongism, my neatly ordered world started to crumble. In August 1985 my mother, along with our son who was then 13, traveled back to Texas to join in the celebration of my Uncle Alvin and Aunt Esther's 50th wedding anniversary. On the way home from a celebratory dinner my mother was killed in an auto accident, along with my Aunt Esther and Uncle Alvin. Our son was not killed in the crash because at the last minute he had decided to go home in a car with some of his cousins. Emotionally shattered, my wife Karen, my daughter and I immediately flew to Texas to join our son and our grieving relatives. We attended the funeral in Needville, Texas, before bringing my mother's body back to California for burial.

Five months later, as I continued to mourn the loss of my mother, Herbert W. Armstrong died. Within a year or two God launched a rescue mission for me, and for that matter, many others within the Worldwide Church of God. Looking back on those dark and painful days, there is no question that the road that took me out of the swamps of *Bad News Religion* was paved with God's amazing grace.

While I was close to Herbert Armstrong, I was even closer to his chosen successor, Joseph Tkach. Within a few years after

Armstrong's death, I started to see and experience God moving in the lives of Joseph Tkach and a few other close friends, as well as in my own.

It was the beginning of my long journey out of the religious badlands. As I grieved over my mother's tragic death, I recalled her claim that we were in a cult. At that time of grief and loss God was using a variety of personal experiences to conclusively demonstrate to me that I could never be good enough to qualify for salvation. One of the frightening realities of religious legalism is that you can never be good enough. God was opening my eyes, through many life experiences, to see the bankruptcy of any system that pretends to impart righteousness through rules and regulations. In my case it took almost 35 years to learn this painful lesson—and even then it was only by God's grace that I escaped.

At the time I didn't know exactly what was wrong, but it soon became obvious to me that eventually I would have to leave Armstrongism. Herbert Armstrong was dead—this one person who had so controlled my life and who had determined how I understood the world. The more I studied and prayed, the more I saw error and heretical teaching.

For some time I was upset with Herbert W. Armstrong. But the more I prayed, the more I believed that I could not place all of the blame at his doorstep, and I still don't. I gave him any power he had exercised over my life. I had to look into the mirror for the person who bore most of the blame. I believe that God gently nudged me in the direction of seeing that wallowing in self-pity and being a victim is living in denial. I had to face myself; not a pretty picture.

As I poured myself into a study of the Bible, and of religion, church history, theology, and apologetics, the picture became even more repulsive. I came to see the dogmatic claims of Armstrongism, a religion that claimed to have all the answers, as bogus. Armstrongism had given me a false identity and a goal and a future that was an illusion. But now, in the late 1980s, each new week of my life brought more insight into the flawed and broken foundation I had lived by— my religious life was falling apart. Once I believed I knew precisely who I was and where I was going. There was a time when I believed the Armstrong version of why I was born. Now I discovered the truth that the house of Armstrongism had been built upon sand (Matthew 7:26–27). Just as Jesus said, it was raining and the winds were blowing and my spiritual house of sand was crumbling.

I never knew my father, though I have always respected his memory. My mother, God bless her, saw to that. Now I came to the painful awareness that I had never known Jesus either. I was a religious professional. My entire life was based upon a cultic version of Christianity. And now, even though I knew the name of Jesus Christ, even though I had memorized and quoted his teachings, even though I had once taught a college class called *Life and Teachings of Jesus,* I realized that I had never known Jesus.

Some time later I heard an anecdote that I have since recited many times. It seems that many years ago a pastor and a famous actor were both invited to a dinner party, and as the dinner progressed the host asked the pastor and the actor to read the same biblical passage. The pastor knew that he was no match for the dramatic talent of the actor and was nervous about being a poor example of his faith. According to the story the actor recited the selected portion of Scripture first, and the guests at the table followed his reading with polite applause.

The pastor then stood and started to read the same passage. When he finished there was silence for a few seconds, and then the dinner guests started to applaud, applause that grew until eventually they rose from their chairs to pay homage to the moving interpretation provided by the pastor.

After dinner the host asked the pastor the secret behind his passionate reading. The pastor simply said, "I know the Author."

It was one of many painful but true realities that started to dawn on me as Jesus took me by the hand to lead me to rest in him. All my life I had been an actor, just reading the script. Of course I didn't think I was acting, but I realized that "religion", apart from God, could give me just so much. The only thing that any religion that is not based on God's grace can do is to help you read your lines, obey the rules and jump through the hoops it prescribes.

When Jesus introduced himself to me, I met the Author. The Author was the Jesus whose name I knew and whose teachings I thought I understood, but I never knew him. The Jesus I never knew was the Jesus about whom I taught thousands of college students over the years, in a class titled *Life and Teachings of Jesus.* Jesus found me, and that's the only way I was able to come to know him, for I was so lost I had no idea where to start looking for him.

Leaving *Bad News Religion* of any size, shape or description is a walk through the valley of the shadow of death. It involves walking by faith, not by sight (2 Corinthians 5:7) and means forsaking the mirage of rules, regulations and rituals that try to assure us of physical evidence that God is happy with us. Legalism is the common virus that affects all of *Bad News Religion*—whether it is a cultic movement that claims to be Christian, or a Christian church that adheres to the essential teachings of Christianity, or a religion that claims no affiliation to Jesus Christ whatsoever. Legalism is the common ingredient. Be more righteous. Be better. Work harder. Give. Serve. Qualify. Improve. Do more. That's what I mean by *Bad News Religion*—there is no "Good News" in it.

God's grace opened my eyes to the real Jesus and the real gospel. His grace gave me, as it were, a road map to find my way out of the swamps of legalism. I started reading *all* of the Bible, not just the passages that were used as "proof texts" by the followers of Armstrongism. When I reached for the hand of my Savior, he helped me out of the swamplands of *Bad News Religion*.

Initially, the authentic gospel of God's grace made me ashamed and angry—ashamed because I had been lost in legalistic swamps for so long and had no clue about the real gospel; angry because grace exalted Jesus and diminished me. Grace was in my face with the powerful and unequivocal message that my good deeds did not amount to nearly enough to satisfy the payment for my sin.

The gospel is, by its very definition, great news. But it wasn't good news for me then! The real gospel of Jesus Christ revealed me to be a pretender, a duped and deluded religious professional whose life and career had been built on a foundation of sand. I faced the pathetic and ugly truth that I had no idea about what I had been preaching and teaching.

2

The Past Is Prelude

"As Kierkegaard says, nothing displeases or revolts us more than New Testament Christianity when it is properly proclaimed. It can neither win millions of Christians nor bring revenues and earthly profits. . . . History bears witness that in generation after generation there has been a highly respected social class (that of priests) whose task it is to make of Christianity the very opposite of what it really is."

—*The Subversion of Christianity,* Jacques Ellul

I MAGINE WAKING UP and finding that what you always accepted as *up* is really *down* and what you have believed to be *left* is actually *right*. Imagine assuming that you were part of the one and only true group of Christians on earth, only to find that you had actually been an enemy of Christ.

I was angry and bitter. As Jesus walked me through that harsh and morose part of the valley of the shadow of death, I started to understand what my grandfather Alex had felt about the old country. He never wanted to talk about his past, and now I didn't either.

I didn't want to talk about who I had been. I wanted to be a brand new person. I didn't want to talk about the old country of the religious swamps and badlands I had inhabited. I wanted it all to be a bad dream. I wanted it to go away.

By God's grace, over the course of several years I slowly came to another painful conclusion. The spiritual reality of new life in Christ is that, while he lives within us and produces his righteousness in us, we still live in this body of flesh. He gives us new life now, on this side of eternity, yet we remain confronted with the daunting challenge of the physical here and now. I discovered that my past framed the reality of who I was, and my past would be part of who I would always be. Like my Grandfather Alex, I wanted to leave the old country behind. But I couldn't, any more than my grandfather could, as hard as he tried. The past had happened. It was real—ugly, nasty, but real.

On the old television program *Mork and Mindy,* Robin Williams played Mork, an alien who had landed on this earth inside of an egg and hatched. Mork had no earthly context, no background and no roots. It was this lack of human history that made for endless hilarity in every episode, as Mork encountered culture and society.

One of the painful but necessary lessons of walking with Christ involves accepting who we used to be and where we have come from. Denial of our past does not obliterate our past. We are not Mork, we all have a past and a context. Our past is prelude. God's grace helped me to accept the reality of my past. Healthy Christians who have been touched and healed by the Great Physician are not in denial. The past is not our present to be sure, but the past happened, whether we like it or not. The great news is that God not only rescues us from our past, he redeems our past. He gives us new life in Christ, a life that does not deny our past, but uses it in a new context.

There is no question that apart from God's grace I would still be treading water, desperately trying to keep my head above the murky waters of *Bad News Religion,* gasping for air and filling my lungs and soul with spiritually toxic swamp gas. That's my past. That was me. Swamp gas Albrecht.

God doesn't hatch us out of a cosmic egg like Mork—he reclaims us from our past, using what we used to be for his own purpose. Part of what we are now, in Christ, is what we used to be. As one of William Faulkner's characters said in *Requiem for a Nun,* "The past is never dead. It's not even past." By his grace God redeems our past and where we have come from for his glory.

Saul became Paul. Chuck Colson of Watergate became Chuck Colson of Prison Fellowship. Augustine the sinner became Augustine, mighty man of God. The past is prelude. It may be painful and embarrassing. It may be ugly. The swamps of *Bad News Religion* have their own distinctive aroma! The past may be the old country we would rather forget. But the past is what we were before—before Christ.

God's amazing grace will take the bad stuff of your life and transform it for his glory and his purpose. No matter how useless and meaningless your past may seem, your past can be redeemed. That's the amazing thing about God. He is in the rescue and reclamation business. He takes useless and lifeless cast-off refuse, trash that no human being can see any use for, and reclaims it. Nothing we have done is beyond his reach. He breathes new life into what is cast off and good for nothing.

Don't deny who you have been or what you have done. You don't need to run away from your past. No matter where you have been, now matter how dark the journey, no matter how ashamed or angry you may be, God will transform you according to his plan for your life. Don't ever let anyone tell you that you are beyond hope. Don't let yourself believe that you have screwed up your life so royally that God is not interested.

Don't let *Bad News Religion* convince you that God is so mad at you that only a lifetime of obedience to religious rules and regulations could ever redeem you from your past. You will simply be exchanging one of the swamps of *Bad News Religion* for another. According to the false gospel of religious legalism, your only hope is to atone for your past by producing a lifetime of good works and meritorious deeds.

Is Grace Too Good to be True?

A pastor friend of mine once told me about a church he was driving by. He noticed a large sign on the front door, and he had to stop for a closer look.

Attention! Behind these doors we worship regularly with liars, thieves, gossips, backbiters, people with troubled marriages, alcoholics, and drug takers. We welcome hypocritical, jealous, envious, coveting, materialistic sinners of all sizes, shapes and colors.

God's amazing grace will take the bad stuff of your life and transform it for his glory and his purpose.

My pastor friend got out of his car and walked up to the door because the next part of the message was in smaller type he could not read from his car.

But the good news is that we all have something in common. We believe that the church, the body of Christ, is a hospital for sinners, not a museum for saints. The Lord, who is our rest, reaches out to save us and brings us together as a community of the saints. We gather here to worship him, to plan how we might be better agents and ambassadors of change in a darkened world that needs good news. You are welcome to join us, but be warned that we take Christianity seriously.

As my friend told me the story, I couldn't help but think about Martin Luther, who also placed a message on a church door. Both of the messages had a common denominator—God's amazing grace.

I will never forget how God intervened in my world to begin teaching me the lesson that the people who worshipped in that church apparently knew. I lived much of my life in a narrow, exclusive, hypercritical, fault-finding religion that judged me and others by our performance. To be honest, I did my best to share (and enforce) the same bad news with others.

I was baptized as an infant in a whitewashed Lutheran church on the Kansas plains. The church and denomination in which I was baptized were grounded in the historical and essential teachings of Christianity. Much later in life I discovered that correct doctrine and biblically based creeds can be infiltrated by *Bad News Religion*. Early in life my faith was hijacked, as I fell under the sway of a mesmerizing, toxic blend of enticing teaching and overbearing legalism.

Grace rescued me from the un-grace of religious rituals and restrictions, from legalism, from prediction addiction (endlessly setting dates for the second coming of Jesus Christ), and from the health and wealth gospel—not to mention a vast eclectic collection of conspiratorial, unbiblical and heretical teachings!

Grace showed me that nothing I had ever done, or that I could ever do, would be enough to convince God to love me and save me. Grace helped me see that nothing I could ever do would atone for my sin.

Grace gently guided me to the cross, a place where I had been taught that only spiritual wimps and lazy, misguided sentimentalists gathered as a last resort. As a true believer, a slave of cultic teaching, I was convinced that people who lacked character, will power, and the drive to overcome their own sins used the cross of Christ as a crutch. Strong Christians, I believed, didn't need the cross. And they certainly didn't need grace!

God's grace helped me see that we humans are not capable of taking care of our own sins. We would rather not humble ourselves before God and admit that we are not capable of taking care of our own spiritual problems. But we all need help—no one is a spiritual superman or superwoman who can produce the righteousness God requires.

Grace opened my eyes to see that performance is at the foundation of all legalism, even when *Bad News Religion* adorns itself with the name of Jesus Christ. When Jesus mercifully took me by the hand to show me the way out of the religious swamp of Armstrongism, at first I thought that my battles with legalism were in the past. I naïvely thought that *Bad News Religion* was contained in the swamps. I soon discovered that while a lethal strain of the virus of legalism inhabits cultic swamps, *Bad News Religion* is everywhere!

God's grace directed me to the true body of Christ and to the historically and biblically accurate teachings and doctrines that identify authentic Christianity. At first I thought that people who attended churches where statements of faith assured alignment with the historic Christian faith would be free of the baggage and barnacles of "churchianity" and legalism.

I found out that there are many detours that lead to the swamplands of religious legalism. Grace showed me that neither creeds nor denominational dogma nor the appropriation of biblical terms and language ensure the teaching and practice of authentic, Christ-centered Christianity.

I am a critic of religious legalism, but more importantly I am a deeply devoted Christian. I am also a recovering legalist, and I know the deadly power of religious legalism. I know that Christ set me free from its bondage. I know that I was blind but now I see (John 9:25). I must report what I see and who healed and rescued me, whether modern religious Pharisees like the implications of my story or not.

Grace helped me see that it is a travesty and a perversion of the gospel of Jesus Christ to be calling oneself a Christian while insisting that the work of salvation is either primarily a human effort or a combination of what Jesus did plus what we accomplish on our own. God's grace denies all heretical ideas and philosophies that proclaim human effort to be necessary to gain God's favor.

My journey out of religious legalism helped me to see the importance of Christians as watchmen at the gates of the kingdom, assisting and supporting the unsuspecting from the deceptive, destructive and divisive world of cults. Cults are born out of the excesses, shortcomings, and flaws of Christianity—and they thrive for the same reason.

Swamps are the breeding ground of viruses, and I found that the virus of religious legalism has seeped inside the gates of the church, attacking and destroying from within. It's an insidious virus because we do not expect churches, pastors, and ministry leaders that seem to say and believe the right things to be in the grip of legalistic bondage. I had several experiences as I left the religious swamps with people that I thought were Christian. They turned out to be just as enslaved to legalistic religion as I had been—just as self-righteous, judgmental, and unforgiving.

Doctrinal fidelity and "being right" can become a point of pride. Several years ago at a Christian Bookseller's Association convention in Atlanta a nationally known Christian leader spoke to the issue of my past, informing me "You're on probation. We'll be watching you." The talk show host who was interviewing both of us responded, "It seems to me that you're giving Greg a similar reception that Saul received just after his experience on the Road to Damascus."

Bad News Religion is spiritual terrorism that relentlessly attacks authentic Christianity, because legalism knows that grace is the mortal enemy of human attempts to win divine favor by merit. That's why there is so much resistance to grace. God's grace threatens the status quo of the world we think we have under control.

- Are you—or someone you love—enslaved by any kind of movement, group, church or denomination that incessantly drives you to do more and more stuff and thereby impress God with your goodness and deeds?
- Are you exhausted by futile attempts to measure up, and frustrated by endless harangues that tell you that you just need to try harder?
- Do you feel like a hamster endlessly running around a wheel inside a cage in a vain attempt to conquer all of your problems so that God will love you?
- Do you think that real Christianity seems to be an irrational, pathetic dog-and-pony show, much like what you have seen on television?
- Do you believe that God clinically judges and records your daily performance and that your salvation is always hanging in the balance?
- Do you believe that God has a giant spiritual scoreboard in heaven, with angels constantly recording and updating your spiritual performance?
- Have you been convinced that God is mad at you and takes some kind of perverse pleasure in dangling your feet over the hot coals of hell?
- Have you allowed some authoritarian, charismatic pastor or leader to have influence and power over you because he or she has a "special anointing"?
- Are you are burned out because of unreasonable legalistic demands?

The incredibly good news is that Jesus Christ can and will make you free. Grace is the unbelievably amazing, beyond belief, almost too-good-to-be-true good news that nothing you can do will make

God love you more than he already does. And, conversely, there is nothing you can do that will make God love you less.

Grace does sound too good to be true—but it is the truth of the gospel of Jesus Christ. Legalistic religion is opposed to grace, because grace will put *Bad News Religion* out of business. Rules-based and performance-centered religion is opposed to grace in much the same way as when Jesus came into the world with grace. Unfortunately, some today who need to escape the world of legalism and its un-Christian demands find themselves returning to the religious swamps in a death march to the unyielding drumbeat of legalism and ritualism. Many refugees from legalism are being marched from one swamp of legalism into another swamp of ritualism.

The pied pipers of legalistic religion will lead you on a lemming-like parade into the muddy waters of despair and ruin. Don't listen to them! It is my prayer that God might use this book to open your eyes and soften your heart, to help rescue a family member or loved one who is trapped, and to help you be on your guard for the lethal virus of *Bad News Religion*.

3

DISCOVERING THE REAL JESUS

"The society Jesus founded has been so unlike Jesus. Think of the blood-thirsty Crusades, the cruel Inquisition, and the history of religious persecution. The church is still so unlike Jesus, and we may well have been scarred by its hypocrisy or bored by its blandness. We recall, maybe, that dreary local church to which we were dragged, protesting, when we were young. Or we reflect on the divisions in the church, the failures of its leadership, and the small difference it seems to make in the lives of its members. Is that why we don't want to know about Jesus?"

—*Who Is This Jesus?*, MICHAEL GREEN

FOR US TO CLEARLY UNDERSTAND and avoid *Bad News Religion*, we must first understand the Good News of the gospel—what authentic Christianity looks like. The real, grace-filled message of the gospel is personified in Jesus. Christianity is a Person, and it is the real Jesus that *Bad News Religion* has failed to proclaim. In *What's Wrong With the World*, G.K. Chesterton said, "Christianity has not been tried and found wanting; it has been found difficult and left untried."

In many cases the real Jesus has been recast into a religious icon that serves the goals of religion. As a result the majority of human beings who believe in God visualize him as difficult to please. They've come to believe he is harsh, unyielding, judgmental, and ungracious. Ironically, this flawed picture of God is a product of Christendom whose fundamental assignment has been to communicate the real Jesus to a world that desperately needs him (Matthew 28:19–20).

Jesus came to reveal the Father (Matthew 11:27). The Eternal Son of God "became flesh and made his dwelling among us" (John 1:14). Jesus said, "Anyone who has seen me has seen the Father" (John 14:9). "God was pleased to have all his fullness dwell in him" (Colossians 1:19). Jesus is "the exact representation" of God (Hebrews 1:3). Discovering authentic Christianity is based upon understanding and knowing the real Jesus. Authentic Christianity reflects the real Jesus, the one whose image has been besmirched and clouded by religious legalism's misrepresentations. The real Jesus, and the authentic Christianity he gives, are buried, like barnacles on a boat, by layers of religious rituals, rules, and regulations.

Christendom has organized Christianity into a regimented system, obscuring the real Jesus with its authoritarian dictates and rites and rituals. The truth is that Jesus constantly opposed the primary religious institution of his day. Christians have often assumed, and in some cases have been assured, that it was the Jewish religion with which Jesus was upset. But this assumption and the resulting false assurances are far from the truth of Scripture. The truth is that the real Jesus always conflicts with religious legalisms of any variety, including permutations of Christianity that appropriate the name of Jesus Christ.

The real Jesus has a message for our world today—a world that is increasingly voting with its feet against the oppressive, rules-dominated overbearing religious culture that claims to speak for God. The real Jesus is a Jesus who is the very antithesis of *Bad News Religion*.

Here's one of the many passages that record Jesus' unequivocal opposition to religious legalism:

> While Jesus was having dinner at Matthew's house, many
> tax collectors and "sinners" came and ate with him and his
> disciples. When the Pharisees saw this, they asked his disci-

ples, "Why does your teacher eat with tax collectors and 'sinners'?" On hearing this, Jesus said, "It is not the healthy who need a doctor, but the sick. But go and learn what this means: 'I desire mercy, not sacrifice.' For I have not come to call the righteous, but sinners."

—MATTHEW 9:10–13

According to Jesus the religious establishment had declared themselves spiritually healthy and assumed they were beyond need of any of the services of the Great Physician. It happened then, and it still happens today. Jesus did not accept their spiritual self-diagnosis. Jesus declared that the unqualified would be freely admitted to his new church, rather than membership granted on the basis of merit—the prevailing status quo of religious admissions policies. Those who had determined that they were immune from the spiritual disease Jesus came to heal did not respond to him. On the other hand, those who were acutely aware of their need flocked to him.

Jesus' life and ministry continually reached those who accepted their vulnerability and their need. One factor that enabled them to clearly see their sorry state was that legalistic religion had rejected them and thus they had not received the full spiritual conditioning that religious legalism offered. They were not as legalistically indoctrinated as religious insiders.

Jesus ministered to these spiritually marginalized religious outcasts. He reversed all the standards of the religion of his day, just as authentic Christianity challenges the prevailing notions of religious traditions and conventions today.

Jesus reserved his most fiery rhetoric for the debilitating impact of performance-based religion. Let's step back and see how Jesus defines *Bad News Religion.* As a way of discovering the real Jesus we can look to his words for direction about the treacherous and subtle devices of legalistic religion and to his example for a role model of authentic Christianity.

JESUS IDENTIFIES BAD NEWS RELIGION

If you are at all familiar with the Gospels, the first four books of the New Testament, you will know that Jesus was popular and well liked by virtually all who knew him (with the exception of the religious establishment). Jesus was God in the flesh, grace personified, a compelling personality, a breath of fresh air. But religious professionals intensely disliked him, and eventually it was this segment of society who saw to it that he was crucified in the prime of his life.

The Pharisees and teachers of the law were highly respected men in the Jewish world to which Jesus came. But it was this group with which Jesus constantly clashed. Virtually every Gospel reference to the Pharisees and the teachers of the law is negative. Jesus called the Pharisees names—he used them as examples of what not to do and how not to behave. Matthew 23 is the one chapter that summarizes Jesus' precise and definitive objections to the religion of the Pharisees. The teaching of the Pharisees was the *Bad News Religion* of Jesus' day—and while the Pharisees he addressed died long ago, the same *Bad News Religion* is enslaving, abusing, exploiting, beguiling, and entrapping millions today.

Verses 2–12 of Matthew 23 are addressed to Jesus' disciples and the larger group who originally listened to Jesus' exposé of legalistic religion. In this first part of the chapter, Jesus speaks of the malicious and toxic teaching of the Pharisees and teachers of the law in the third person. In verses 13–36 Jesus gets up close and personal as he directly confronts religious leaders of that day. The subject that Jesus passionately attacks throughout the chapter is *Bad News Religion*.

Isaiah has a message we would do well to consider as we ponder Jesus' scathing denunciation:

> This is the one I esteem: he who is humble and contrite in spirit, and trembles at my word.

—ISAIAH 66:2

We do not wade into Matthew 23 for the purpose of throwing stones, but to allow the words of God to penetrate our world and reality. We seek his truth, and we search for his heart and mind. As Christians we yearn for Christ's mind to live in us (Philippians 2:5) and for his light to shine in our lives. The more I study this portion of Scripture the more amazed I am at the outrage that Jesus expressed toward religiosity.

The Real Jesus is a Jesus who is the very antithesis of *Bad News Religion.*

Matthew 23 is a disturbing chapter—these words are of grave concern to me. This is an indictment of the way I was—reading it propels me to continually yield to Christ so that I may never be found guilty again, as indeed I have been in the past, of proclaiming a *different gospel—which is really no gospel at all* (Galatians 1:6–7).

After all, here is God in the flesh, very man and very God, expressing indignation in the strongest possible terms toward my profession. He is not talking primarily about plumbers, soldiers, clerks, accountants, or salespeople. He is talking about pastors, ministers, denominational administrators, church boards, and ministry leaders. He's talking to Christian authors, theologians, and evangelists. Of course he's talking to the entire world, and then more specifically to all of us who bear the name of Christ, warning us about *Bad News Religion*. But he's directly speaking to the purveyors of *Bad News Religion*.

The line from the old *Pogo* comic strip is ringing in my mind as I type these words on my keyboard—"We have met the enemy and he is us." We should ask Jesus to help us apply these words to ourselves rather than assuming that he is talking about others.

Here's a summary of our Lord's piercing no-holds-barred invective in Matthew 23 that is directed at legalistic religion. Practitioners and proponents of *Bad News Religion*:

- Do not practice what they preach. They are hypocrites who insist on impossible standards, which neither they nor their followers can satisfy (v. 3).
- Oppress those they "serve" by requiring heavy spiritual burdens while excusing themselves from such tyranny. They multiply religious rules as a means of controlling the masses (v. 4). The heavy burdens they impose are in direct contrast with the easy yoke and light burden offered by Jesus (11:28–30).
- Wallow in the adulation of the crowds who defer to them and heap religious honor and accolades upon them (v. 5).
- Love to hear their full religious titles, scholarly accomplishments, and academic degrees and to experience the respect that accompanies them. They are status seekers, not servants (v. 7–12).
- Actually prevent people from entering the kingdom of heaven, the absolute antithesis of their job description (v. 13). They place a price on admission to the kingdom of God, a kingdom that God gives by his grace.

- Exhaust all resources in enlarging their spiritually perverse domain and dominion by winning new converts. Growth of their church or ministry is for the purpose of elevating and exalting themselves, with little or no concern for the spiritual well being of proselytes who become *twice as much a son of hell* as they are (v. 15).
- Have distorted values, obsessing upon monetary matters that may materially enrich their own lives while missing justice, mercy and faithfulness (v. 23, see also Micah 6:8). They are narrow-minded, blind spiritual guides who miss the big picture.
- Are exclusively focused on externals while failing to address internal spiritual needs (v. 25–28).
- Fight, persecute and kill true messengers of God (v. 33–34).

FIVE HALLMARKS OF AUTHENTIC CHRISTIANITY

Authentic Christianity looks like Jesus. Christ is the head of his body of believers, and the authentic body of Christ obviously bears a striking resemblance to its head. Consider five hallmarks of the life of Jesus, the founder of Christianity, the risen Lord who continues to empower believers everywhere. These five hallmarks are of course not a definitive list but they are five Christ-centered signposts that stand in stark contrast to legalism. As we contrast God's grace with religious legalism these five hallmarks can help us to focus on the central and foundational issues of Christianity.

1) *Love.* Jesus' life, teachings and ministry were characterized by love —by unselfish, unconditional love. To be in the presence of Jesus meant to be accepted, ministered to, comforted, directed, instructed, and provided for. Love was, and is, the primary distinctive of

authentic Christianity. God's love, exemplified in Jesus, is a new kind of love, an extra-human kind of love. It's not the love of self-gratification or human emotion. God's love does not rely on human feeling. God's love is not subject to or defined by human criteria. It is a love that we can know and give only through Jesus who lives his life within us.

Love is perhaps the supreme attribute of God. God's love springs from the very essence of who he is. Two Greek words for love are frequently used in the New Testament—*agape* and *philia*. *Philia* is a love of affection and friendship that is earned, given on the basis of merit and worth. *Agape* is a love that is given without regard to right, entitlement or merit. God extends *agape* to us without qualification, in spite of the fact that we are unworthy of it.

> A new command I give you: Love one another. As I have loved you, so you must love one another. By this all men will know that you are my disciples, if you love one another.
> —JOHN 13:34–35

Paul tells us how the love of God was expressed through Jesus at great cost:

> For you know the grace of our Lord Jesus Christ, that though he was rich, yet for your sakes he became poor, so that you through his poverty might become rich.
> —2 CORINTHIANS 8:9

2) *Grace.* In some way all of these five hallmarks of authentic Christianity are subsets of God's love. But grace is not merely another way of understanding God's love, it is an avenue or vehicle through which God's love is given. Grace is all about God's generosity, his

unfaltering, unlimited, extravagant giving. The unbelievable riches of God's grace are further underlined by the fact that God's grace is costly on his part and undeserved on ours. Paul refers to God's grace as an *indescribable gift* in 2 Corinthians 9:15. Authentic Christianity is characterized by gracious acts of mercy and love.

Jesus, who was the very personification of grace, did not lead anyone to believe in what some today call "easy-believism." Jesus told the woman who was taken in the act of adultery, after saving her from being stoned to death, to "Go now and leave your life of sin" (John 8:11). Jesus himself faced temptations as we do, battling sin without ever once giving in (Hebrews 2:18).

But Jesus never yelled, forced, coerced, or bullied people into changing their lives. We search in vain for any example of intimidation or manipulation on the part of Jesus. He didn't quarrel or cry out (Matthew 12:19), he released the oppressed and proclaimed liberty to those who were enslaved (Luke 4:18–19). Jesus wooed people, he drew people and he won them by his gracious and compassionate nature. This is authentic Christianity.

Mercy is often used as a synonym for grace, but while they are related they are two different sides of the same coin. God's grace allows us to receive something that we do not deserve, while God's mercy ensures that we do not receive punishment or a penalty we do deserve.

3) *Service.* No human life has ever come close to producing the level or degree of service that typified the life of Jesus. People flocked to Jesus because they sensed his attentiveness to their concerns. Jesus listened. He nurtured. He cared. Jesus provided physical food and spiritual food. He delivered and healed those who suffered physically, and provided the ultimate Answer for those who were tortured and enslaved by *Bad News Religion.*

Jesus was the prophesied Suffering Servant of Isaiah who

a) voluntarily suffered on our behalf (Isaiah 53:4), b) endured indignities and contempt (Isaiah 49:7; 50:6), c) justified the entire world (Isaiah 42:6; 53:11), d) was pierced, crushed, oppressed, and afflicted for us (Isaiah 53:5-8), and e) extended justice for all nations (Isaiah 42:1,4).

The night before his crucifixion Jesus served his disciples at a meal that has become a sacrament for Christians—Communion, the Lord's Supper. The same night he washed their feet, they were not asked to wash his. And then, as the Lamb of God, he voluntarily went to his cross as the supreme and unmatched act of love.

> Do you understand what I have done for you?" he asked them. "You call me 'Teacher' and 'Lord,' and rightly so, for that is what I am. Now that I, your Lord and Teacher, have washed your feet, you also should wash one another's feet. I have set you an example that you should do as I have done for you. I tell you the truth, no servant is greater than his master, nor is a messenger greater than the one who sent him. Now that you know these things, you will be blessed if you do them.
>
> —JOHN 13:12–17

The mother of two of the disciples once asked Jesus if her sons could have the two top executive-level positions under Jesus in his kingdom. The rest of the disciples were, needless to say, unhappy about this request that, if Jesus granted it, would have effectively relegated them to lesser positions. Jesus used their indignation to teach them about service. The Good News of the gospel is not about power and privilege, it is about service.

> You know that the rulers of the Gentiles lord it over

them, and their high officials exercise authority over them. Not so with you. Instead, whoever wants to become great among you must be your servant, and whoever wants to be first must be your slave—just as the Son of Man did not come to be served, but to serve, and to give his life as a ransom for many.

—MATTHEW 20:25–28

4). *Humility.* Here's an attribute that stands out in our world of self-promotion and pride. Jesus' birth, the watershed event of all human history, was remarkably unheralded. No marching bands and no pageantry. It all took place in a backwater town, far from the center of downtown Jerusalem. Jesus arrived in Jerusalem riding on a lowly colt. No procession of chauffeur driven limousines, just a lowly colt. No chariot with prancing war horses, just a lowly colt.

God requires that we walk with justice, that we love mercy, and walk with humility (Micah 6:8). Religious pride opposes humility, for apart from authentic Christianity religion is fueled by power and performance. Humility accepts our human dependence on God, and is grateful for his grace. Jesus taught that only those who become like little children would enter the kingdom of heaven (Matthew 18:3–4).

If you have any encouragement from being united with Christ, if any comfort from his love, if any fellowship with the Spirit, if any tenderness and compassion, then make my joy complete by being like-minded, having the same love, being one in spirit and purpose.

Do nothing out of selfish ambition or vain conceit, but in humility consider others better than yourselves. Each of you should look not only to your own interests, but also to

the interests of others. Your attitude should be the same as
that of Christ Jesus . . . .

—PHILIPPIANS 2: 1–5

5). *Joy.* Authentic Christianity is filled with happiness and joy.
Christians have, after all, been given the pearl of great price
(Matthew 13:46). We have stumbled upon a treasure hidden in a
field (Matthew 13:44). We are heirs of God's kingdom and his glory
(Romans 8:17). We have been saved and redeemed, and we are given
the riches of his grace (Ephesians 2:7). Deep, abiding joy character-
izes authentic Christianity, for we have been given victory through
Jesus Christ our Lord (1 Corinthians 15:57).

Joy is produced in us by God the Holy Spirit (Galatians 5:22). Joy
is centered in God rather than human self-interest. Joy that is a gift
of God runs deeper than mere human pleasure and gratification. In
fact, God's joy can exist in spite of external, physical problems that
bring pain and suffering.

Empowered by joy, authentic Christians don't take themselves
too seriously, but they are resolute and unyielding in their worship
of Jesus Christ. Authentic Christians are not lifeless killjoys who
oppose fun and laughter, but are people who have the assurance of
salvation, given to them through the presence of the risen Lord.
Authentic Christianity is filled with joy because its focus is on the
Savior, rather than on *Bad News Religion.*

Jesus did not stand aloof from sinful humanity, he engaged himself in his society and culture. He loved everyone, finding joy and
purpose in helping and reaching out to all who were in need. As the
Light of this world, he radiated joy and happiness. His teachings
were filled with humor, as so carefully explained in *The Humor of
Christ,* by Elton Trueblood. Explaining Jesus as the *radiance of God's*

glory and the exact representation of his being (Hebrews 1:3), the author of Hebrews says:

> You have loved righteousness and hated wickedness; there-
> fore God, your God, has set you above your companions by
> anointing you with the oil of joy.
>
> —HEBREWS 1:9

In the following chapters, we will look at the many facets of God's grace—God's grace described by love, generosity, mercy, compassion, humility, service, and joy. We will examine and contrast grace with legalism from many configurations and perspectives. We will consider objections to grace and discover what happens when God's amazing grace collides with the requirements and demands of legalistic religion. As we compare God's amazing grace with religious legalism may God allow us to appreciate and "grasp how wide and long and high and deep is the love of Christ..." (Ephesians 3:18).

The cross of Christ means that all that we do falls short of God's perfection, and that nothing we do, be it a vice or a virtue, changes his love for us or his willingness to accept us.

4

JUST WHAT DO YOU MEAN . . . BAD NEWS RELIGION?

"If the divine call does not make us better, it will make us very much worse. Of all bad men, religious bad men are the worst."

—*Reflections on the Psalms,* C. S. LEWIS

THE SPIRITUALLY LETHAL VIRUS of legalism that attacks God's grace can be found in any belief system or structure that promises God's blessings in return for human efforts and performance. *Bad News Religion* is based on the conviction that if we do more and try harder we will be able to manipulate and obligate God into accepting our good deeds as at least partial payment for our salvation. The hypothesis of *Bad News Religion* is that our performance of religious duties and obedience to religious laws gains us a higher standing with God than we would have otherwise enjoyed.

This toxic virus is present in all world religions, in fact it is the common denominator in all of them. The lie that humans can control their own eternal destiny by their attempts to be righteous and by their diligence in avoiding evil is the common thread.

Hindus have their obligatory prayer wheels and ritual cleansing in the Ganges, Muslims have prescribed daily prayers that must be given at specific times, required pilgrimages to Mecca and dietary restrictions. In primitive animism, legalism exacts its pound of flesh in practices that demand food to be left for household spirits and that compel the use of amulets to repel evil spirits.

By contrast, authentic Christianity proclaimed by the gospel of Jesus Christ is unique among all religions in that it offers a completely different dimension in our human quest for salvation. The genius of Christianity is not its unique doctrines nor its unequalled ceremonies, but the deity of Jesus. Because of Jesus, humans are saved from the religiosity of believing that they must save themselves by producing good deeds.

This is a dramatic difference, causing many Christians to claim that real Christianity is not actually a religion at all; it's more accurately defined as a personal relationship with Jesus Christ. That claim and definition is biblically accurate and offers no room for the obligations and religious enslavement of *Bad News Religion*. However, the fact remains that when most people use the term *religion,* authentic Christianity is included in the generic definition.

Therefore, as authentic Christians we should not insist on a definition of religion that is not understood by the world at large, but instead we must seek to share the good news of the gospel in a way that those who are infected by the virus of *Bad News Religion* can comprehend. The real issue that authentic Christians must face is the fact that much of Christendom has been infiltrated and even co-opted by legalism, and therefore has degenerated into just another religion. The sad truth for many is that their relationship with their legally incorporated denomination and congregation or their relationship with the human leadership of their church is actually far more real and significant than their relationship with Jesus. Simply claiming that we have a personal relationship with Jesus does not grant us immunity from *Bad News Religion*.

Authentic Christianity places Jesus at the very center and core of Christianity. According to the gospel of Jesus Christ, Jesus alone is the foundation of salvation. All salvation flows through him and from him. Because of Jesus' cross, and the righteousness he produced, we are saved by grace. God's goodness and grace saves us, not our own works.

Christendom at large has been and continues to be corrupted by the heady and intoxicating idea that we humans can make a contribution to our salvation. We humans are suckers for religion, which assures us that our efforts will have a significant impact upon our salvation.

Legalism in Disguise

Legalism often adorns itself in a Christian uniform, and as a part of that disguise it talks the talk, paying lip service to God's grace. Christ-centered words and terms that apply exclusively to the gospel of grace are employed, but new meaning is poured into them. Legalism uses biblical words and phrases but re-defines them in an attempt to cover its true nature. Legalistic rhetoric about grace often goes something like this: "Of course we are saved by grace. But what does God expect us to do once he saves us? Can we please him simply by taking advantage of his good graces? Is God like some permissive parent who will give us everything we want and need no matter what we do? No! God will not be taken advantage of!"

The message continues, "It doesn't make sense to believe that God will continue to forgive us, no matter what we do. Yes, he saves us by his grace, but from that point on we have our part to play. We must remain in his good graces. God gets us started. He primes the pump, but from that point on he expects us to prove to him how much we love him, and how much we appreciate his grace. God will love us more if we please him with our dedication and achievements."

Have you ever heard preaching or teaching like that? This approach is not the sole property of cultic groups that teach doctrinal heresy. This kind of do-it-yourself perversion of Christianity has invaded churches whose doctrine seems to be compatible with the core teaching of the historic body of Christ.

The cross of Christ means that all that we do falls short of God's perfection, and that nothing we do, be it a vice or a virtue, changes his love for us or his willingness to accept us.

When grace is preached many pastors feel obligated, sometimes by congregational pressures and expectations, to "balance" a series of messages on grace with another series on holiness. "After all," goes the thinking, "we don't want the congregation to overdose on grace. Where would that lead? They might abuse their freedom in Christ." God does call us to holiness and good character, but it is never given as a precondition to our standing in Christ. The shift from grace to works often leaves the hearer focusing on striving to be good enough to please God, and that is *Bad News Religion*.

Given the prevailing assumption that a little grace is good but too much can be hazardous to your spiritual health, "old fashioned" holiness preaching often immediately follows a message of grace with a legalistic counterpunch that brings a congregation back to its senses. Such preaching centers on external acts and behaviors that we humans do or don't do, and, given such an emphasis, is an absolute contradiction to the gospel of Jesus Christ that is based upon faith alone, grace alone, and Christ alone. Some holiness preaching soft-pedals the legalism by stressing that we need to "live for God" and "please God." But the end result of a soft, politically correct version of legalism is the same when the rubber hits the road—it's up to us to perform, because God bases his love, forgiveness, and mercy upon our good works.

Let me tell you about Susan and Randal. They are a young couple with two pre-school age children who left an extremely legalistic mega-church—an ungracious church that, of all things, included "grace" as a part of its name. They finally found a new church home, a much smaller congregation that claimed to be a safe haven from legalism. Everything seemed to be fine, until they missed a "required" assembly.

Congregational leadership had decided that all members must attend and actively participate in a Christmas celebration worship service. Susan and Randal did not show up. That's when the religious walls started closing in on them. They received some "visitations," when elders came to their home to chide them about their lack of support and involvement. The counseling became an intimidating inquisition, with the question finally being posed, "Do you understand church discipline?"

For Susan and Randal this was legalism déjà vu. Same song, different verse. They would not surrender their freedom in Christ, and therefore sent a letter informing the church that they should no longer be considered members.

Preaching and teaching that judges Christians solely upon external actions almost inevitably leads to manipulation for the purpose of creating guilt and shame. A heavy, unremitting emphasis on sin, defined merely as bad behavior is a one-way road that leads to legalism. In fact, we must also repent of our attempts at earning God's favor through good deeds, as well as our bad deeds. An obsessive concentration on overcoming sinful actions expects unattainable standards of conduct and in turn sets us up for failure. Once we experience the inevitable failure, authoritarian "church discipline" applies the *coup de grace* of guilt and shame. And once individuals are manipulated into a state of shame and guilt, legalism has its way with them.

Holiness preaching, a staple of American fundamentalism, almost always exclusively defines sin as an external behavior. Such preaching and teaching often accentuates the relationship with a church, congregation, pastor or charismatic leader at the expense of the believer's personal relationship with Jesus Christ. To the degree that externalism completely defines our view of sin we move deeper into legalistic religion and further away from the cross of Christ.

Strict rule keeping leads us away from God, not the other way around. The deception of legalism is this: The greater we denounce and declare war upon external sinful actions, the closer we are to God. The truth of the gospel is this: The greater the emphasis on humans earning God's favor by avoiding external sinful deeds the greater our distance from God's amazing grace.

Let me put it this way—it is possible to be the church member of the year simply on the basis of conforming to all of the codes and standards of your denomination and congregation, while at the same time being filled with greed, hatred, lust, and envy. Legalistic religion cannot change the heart—only God can do that.

Bad News Religion causes us to obsess about being right. The more we are convinced that we are right, the more we change the emphasis of the gospel from "change me" to "change them."

Revivals and crusades can be yet another legalistic manipulation in which religiosity can pervert the gospel. Revivals are often dedicated to urging individuals to stop sinning, for the express purpose of convincing God to start doing something we think he needs to be doing.

For example, within the past few decades many churches and ministries have started to preach a "take back America" message, a revival that is based upon "reclaiming" the Godly heritage of America. It's an attractive appeal clothed in patriotism. It seems right, it feels right, but the truth is the idea of taking back America is primarily based upon external works, deeds and behavior. Here's the premise of this message: "We're right because we're doing all the right things, they're wrong because they're doing all the wrong things. They need to change. Let's get this nation back to the way it used to be."

The foundational underpinnings of the "let's get back to the good old days" movement is that America is far more perverted and steeped in sin today than it ever has been. So, the reasoning goes, if we reclaim and recapture the way it used to be, then we would root out much of the sin that pervades our country today. There is no doubt that much is wrong with our culture today. But "getting back to the good old days" will not solve the problem of sin—even if everyone could agree about exactly which era exemplified this mythical standard we are supposed to reclaim. Getting back to the good old days is just another repackaged version of externalism.

Taking back America assumes that the standard we should recapture is some never-never land, *Little House on the Prairie,* perfect world. But history books paint an entirely different picture of our past. There were about the same number of abortions in 1860 as there are today. Murder rates in the 1930s matched our present rates. In 19th century America the age of sexual consent in some states was nine or ten. Prior to the 1920s no laws existed that required a father who divorced or deserted his family to pay child support. Dean Merrill exposes these and many other wrong-headed notions about the "way we were" in his superb book, *Sinners in the Hands of an Angry Church.*

Zeal to roll back the clock to some nonexistent golden age of morality is a legalistic smoke screen that keeps our focus and the spotlight on what we do, rather than on God's grace. Legalism urges us to reclaim some past pinnacle of human achievement—God's grace concentrates our attention to the future glory God will reveal.

So where do we get the idea that we can reclaim or recapture or take back America by our programs and initiatives? The theory that God will reward us when we perform certain duties and refuse to engage in other conduct is not a part of the gospel. It's just one of the many legalistic barnacles that deny the power of God's grace by suggesting that God needs our help.

LEGALISM WANTS TO ENSLAVE YOU!

My experience with cultic legalism has heightened my sensitivity to this watering down of the gospel, this pollution of God's amazing grace. Why do so many continue to fall in this trap? *Bad News Religion* is both popular and successful because it is a part of the human condition. It's the default to which we humans revert. It's the way we are programmed. It makes common sense, which in this case is the diametric opposite of biblical teaching.

Legalism enslaves you by convincing you of what you are already inclined to believe. Your deeds, your power, your performance, your contributions, and your effort are capitalized upon by *Bad News Religion*. It beguiles you by making you feel important. It attacks your spiritual Achilles heel.

God's grace is the only answer for legalism, and it demands our complete surrender and allegiance to Jesus Christ. All humans, religious and secular, are programmed for rewards and punishment behavior. It's part of the human condition. Apart from Christ, all humans live in one of the swamps of religion gone wrong. The only way of escape is to be lifted, by God's grace, to a higher level. Paul described his escape from the swamps, *I have been crucified with Christ and I no longer live, but Christ lives in me* (Galatians 2:20).

Accepting Jesus Christ means that we must renounce the *works* of the flesh —that doesn't just mean rejecting the sins of the flesh, it means forsaking anything and everything that we believe has merit or worth as a contribution to our salvation. What we were dies, it's crucified with Christ, and he now lives his risen life within us. That's the only way out of the swamps.

According to *Bad News Religion,* humans need to repent of vices and make every effort to overcome them and avoid them. According to the cross of Christ, Christians must repent of both our vices and our virtues. If you are mired in some religious swamp, your own presumed virtues may be a real obstacle that prevents you from accepting Jesus Christ. The cross of Christ means that all that we do falls short of God's perfection, and that nothing we do, be it a vice or a virtue, changes his love for us or his willingness to accept us.

We Christians need a reformation—we need to return to Jesus Christ. Forget about taking back America, let's take back our churches and reclaim them from this corruption that envelops them. Christendom is carrying so much baggage that we lose sight of Jesus. We need to return to Jesus Christ alone, and leave the religious stuff behind.

> Therefore, since we are surrounded by such a great cloud of witnesses, let us throw off everything that hinders and the sin that so easily entangles, and let us run with perseverance the race marked out for us. Let us fix our eyes on Jesus, the author and perfecter of our faith. . . .
>
> —HEBREWS 12:1–2

Jesus must be the absolute center of all of our preaching and proclamation. Of course we need to reject sin, and that would first and foremost include anything that takes our focus away from Jesus. This includes both "bad" sins and "good" sins—those sins that are attempts on our part to earn the favor and grace of God in some way by doing "good deeds." *Bad News Religion* is itself a deadly sin and sworn enemy of God's grace. *Bad News Religion* attacks God's grace, diminishing and devaluing the cross of Christ while at the same time enshrining and glorifying human effort and achievement. What Jesus asks us to do or allows us to do after he has saved us is not even worthy to be mentioned in the same breath with the power and majesty of God's grace. We need grace—not legalism.

CHAPTER FOUR—REVIEW AND RECAP

A common virus. *Bad News Religion* is not only present in all world religions, it is the common denominator in all of them.

Religion or relationship? While most people consider Christianity to be a religion, authentic Christianity is actually not a religion, but rather a personal relationship with God. Religion promises God's blessings in return for human efforts, holding out the hope that the performance of duties and deeds gain humans a higher standing with God than they would have otherwise enjoyed—a claim that is not even close to the message proclaimed by the gospel.

Watering down Christianity. *Bad News Religion* has infiltrated much of Christendom, so that it has become just another religion.

God will love us more. Legalism teaches us that God will love us more if we try to please him with our obedience and rule-keeping. In reality, God cannot love us more than he already does.

Take back America? Some Christians believe they must "take back America" in order to return the country to a more virtuous state. The real need is for Christians to return to Jesus—to take back their churches from both *Bad News Religion* and permissiveness.

Repenting of vices and virtues. According to *Bad News Religion*, humans need to repent of their vices. According to authentic Christianity we must repent of both our vices and our virtues. The only virtues that really matter come from God, not from our efforts.

5

ALL YOU NEED IS GRACE!

*"Grace is something you can never get but only be given. There's no way to earn it or deserve it or bring it about any more than you can deserve the taste of raspberries and cream or earn good looks or bring about your own birth. . . . A crucial eccentricity of the Christian faith is the assertion that people are saved by grace. There's nothing **you** have to do. There's nothing you **have** to do. There's nothing you have to **do.**"*

—*Wishful Thinking*, FREDERICK BUECHNER

JUST A FEW YEARS AGO George Harrison, still a young man in his late 50's, died of cancer. Over 40 years ago Harrison was one of four young men from Liverpool, England, who, calling themselves the Beatles, took the world of popular music by storm. After his death the news media quoted friends and relatives who said that Harrison spent a great deal of time in his last years looking for God.

As I read about George Harrison's quest for God I couldn't help considering whether Harrison had fulfilled the truth of a refrain from an old Beatles song titled "Help":

> When I was younger, so much younger than today,
> I never needed anybody's help in any way.
> But now those days are gone, I'm not so self-assured. . .

George Harrison's death affected me in at least two ways. As a long time fan of the Beatles I knew that he was only a few years older than I. When I read the obituaries and I read of the deaths of people who are about the same age as I am, my own mortality comes into sharp focus. Second, I was fascinated to hear that George Harrison was looking for God in his last years on earth. It seems that my own search for God has intensified as I have aged—or perhaps it's been that God's gracious efforts to find me have intensified.

As we get older we gradually deteriorate physically as mortality begins to have its way with us. We become more dependent and less independent. We become much less self-assured about our own abilities and capabilities.

But there are positive benefits of aging, some of them directly related to diminished physical capacity. As we begin to lose the beauty, strength, and "glory" of our physical bodies, it's a little easier to realize that this life is not all there is. The mere process of getting older can help bring God's amazing grace into sharper focus.

God appears to have sharpened Paul's focus on grace as Paul battled with what he simply calls "a thorn in the flesh." Paul explains that he had pleaded with God to take this physical impediment from him, but that God had answered him,

> My grace is sufficient for you, for my power is made perfect in weakness.
>
> —2 CORINTHIANS 12:9

There's that word *grace*. Paul discovered that God's grace was sufficient for him. By God's grace, I am beginning to appreciate the sufficiency of God's grace. God's grace is all I need. I don't need religion, rituals, pills, or potions. I assure you—God's grace is all you need. Notice how Paul responds to God's answer to him.

Therefore I will boast all the more gladly about my weaknesses, so that Christ's power may rest on me. That is why, for Christ's sake, I delight in weaknesses, in insults, in hardships, in persecutions, in difficulties. For when I am weak, then I am strong.

—2 Corinthians 12:9–10

It's the timeless message of Jesus' resurrection. Institutionalized religious legalism (not the Jews and not the Romans) tortured and killed Jesus' body, but *Bad News Religion* could not keep his body in the tomb. As the cornerstone of our faith and the evidence of God's grace that lives within us, the resurrection of Jesus Christ teaches us that our salvation has been won on the cross and that the future resurrection of our bodies is assured because of the empty tomb—not because of our actions, behaviors, rituals, or deeds. Grace is all we need.

The "Best" Christians?

Bad News Religion inevitably leads us to place our faith in external trappings, things we can see and things we can do. It places stress upon how we humans can produce, change, or manipulate our lives—and those of others. Legalistic religion will persuade us to consider the things we can do that will convince God to heal us of physical ailments. Performance-based religion entices us into silly games such as praying precise words and phrases, somewhat like a magic formula, convincing us that if we do what needs to be done then God will answer our prayers the way we want him to.

Religious externalism convinces us that nonessential issues, such as the determination of a precise date for the second coming of Jesus, are of vital importance. Conscientious rule keeping will cause us to obsess about how we can save our necks by doing all the right things to qualify for the Rapture, so we won't be left behind.

Grace is the unseen power of God at work in the lives of those who accept Jesus as sufficient and enough—and sadly God's grace is often diminished or even dismissed by the external emphasis of religion.

Years ago I remember thinking that the best and most deeply converted Christians were those who seemed to be in control of their lives, who walked straight and tall and who seemed to be models of perfection. Even as a young pastor, I thought that God must have specially chosen some of these people who outwardly appeared to have remarkable courage and conviction, so that they could build character through their virtues and show the world by their obedience what Christianity was all about. I was impressed with these talented men and women and what they were able to accomplish.

I have learned that God doesn't call the qualified, he qualifies the called. Fact is, God doesn't call anyone who is qualified—he never has. Such human beings don't exist!

God has gently directed me to see that the people I admired were just as flawed as I was and as I still am. God's grace rips the veneer off the cheap imitation, exposing it as a fraudulent deception. In fact, legalism does not permit its followers to admit to any imperfection, forcing them to live a lie. Because of the lies of legalism many of its followers never realize that religious externalism is an illusion, a spiritual mirage, the religious equivalent of the Emperor's new clothes.

As the years have gone by, and as God has mercifully worked in my life, I have become far more impressed with what Jesus has already done than I am by human efforts to produce righteous deeds.

At this point in my spiritual pilgrimage I am blessed to know many mature Christians who are not rich in this world's goods and who suffer physical pain and hardship in their bodies. These men and women of God are usually not recognized or honored by our society for their brains, brawn, money, or good looks.

But God knows them. God recognizes them. God knows those who have *received his grace.* These wonderful children of God are often not physically impressive. They have learned to depend upon God for everything. They are weak, but God has made them strong.

These men and women of faith I know and know of are still plagued with their thorns in the flesh. For some reason they haven't been able to receive the "special-healing anointing" like the one once offered by a televangelist who claimed that he received such an "anointing" directly from Jesus when he was transported to the throne of God. These men and women of faith have suffered strokes, fought cancers, and are crippled—all because, some would lead us to believe, they have not yet visited the local revival center, or traveled to some shrine or been cleansed by a "holy" river.

The empty tomb reminds us that Christ is not there anymore, but that he is risen, he is alive, he has conquered all religion—and he lives to give us freedom from the deadly virus of legalism.

These men and women of faith that I know are not famous. Their faces are rarely seen on Christian cable TV, nor are their voices often heard on Christian radio. Few of them write books or pastor mega-churches. God knows them as his children, but they are virtually invisible to the world at large. While they can be an embarrassment to the externalism so highly prized by legalism, God embraces and loves them.

In his book *Fresh Faith*, author Jim Cymbala says it well. "The greatest Christian is not the one who has *achieved* the most but rather the one who has *received* the most." Every version and permutation of religion, even those that masquerade as authentic Christianity, places a premium on the works and virtues we humans can produce. Legalism is based on what we do—Christianity is based on what Christ has done.

One of the most effective ways to counter the devious, seductive onslaught of legalism in our lives is to center our faith, practice, and devotion in the cross of Christ.

The cross of Christ is the sign of the end of a relationship with performance-based religion, and the beginning of a relationship with God. The cross of Christ is the sign that our relationship with God is no longer defined by externals but by the internal working of God in our hearts and minds.

THE DIFFERENCE BETWEEN THE OLD AND NEW COVENANTS

For Christians, the heart of God's amazing grace lies in the difference between the Old and New Covenants. The book of Hebrews contrasts the two, continually pointing to the superiority of the New Covenant in Christ. Hebrews insists that God's grace is sufficient for us. God's grace is all we need!

Hebrews teaches one of the foundational lessons of real Christianity—God does for us what we cannot do for ourselves. This book bases much of its teaching upon the earlier writings of Paul in his second letter to the Corinthian church. In 2 Corinthians 3:3–18 Paul compares and contrasts the two covenants:

The Old Covenant:	The New Covenant:
Written with ink (v. 3)	Written with the Spirit (v. 3)
Of the letter (v. 6)	Of the Spirit (v. 6)
The letter kills (v. 6)	The Spirit gives life (v. 6)
Brings condemnation (v. 9)	Brings righteousness (v. 9)
Was once glorious (v. 10)	Glory remains and lasts (v. 11)
Veils the heart (v. 14-15)	Takes the veil away (v. 16)

Hebrews insists that Christ is superior to the religion and rituals of Judaism (or, by implication, any religion) and its requirements. Hebrews demonstrates that the New Covenant Jesus gave is founded on better promises (8:6). Hebrews teaches that if there were "nothing wrong" with the Old Covenant, there would have been no reason for the new (8:7). Hebrews says that the old is "obsolete," and, written just a few years before the destruction of the Temple in Jerusalem that was so central in Judaism, predicts that requirements to keep the Old Covenant would "soon disappear" (8:13).

The Old Covenant, in some form, is often the authority churchianity appeals to in an attempt to "improve" Christianity, to "organize" God, and to make Christians "better." Hebrews explains what is important and what is not important for Christians. Hebrews leads us to authentic Christianity, distinguishing it from religion based upon externals.

The tenth chapter of Hebrews contrasts Christ's sacrifice on the cross—and his perfect atonement for our sins—with the endless cycle of rituals and animal sacrifices under the Old Covenant. Christ's sacrifice is once and for all (9:25–26).

As our High Priest, Jesus forgave sin once and for all—something the priests of the Old Covenant could never do. But legalism uncompromisingly insists on its priests, potions, and philosophies, which poison God's grace.

Some Christians believe that God will not forgive us unless and until we ask God to forgive our each and every specific sin. Others believe that we must personally confess to a human who will, in turn, forgive our sin as God's representative. Where do we get these ideas? Not from the Bible. Not from the gospel of Jesus Christ.

There was one piece of furniture missing in the Jews' tabernacle and later in their temple: no chair. No place to sit down. The lesson? The work of the priests of Israel, the priests of the Old Covenant, was never done. It is impossible for human beings to ever do enough things to atone for their own sins. There was not enough time in the priests' workday to offer a sufficient number of sacrifices to make the nation of Israel righteous.

Michael Green explains the background that the book of Hebrews is addressing:

> Judaism in the first century was dominated by three things: the temple at Jerusalem, with all its ritual sacrifices; the Sabbath day, around which an overwhelming burden of prohibitions had gathered; and the law of God, originally given to Moses on Mount Sinai and written down in the Old Testament but interpreted in minute detail by the clergy of the day. Temple, law, Sabbath—these three. If you wanted to please God, this was the threefold route you must tread. You must go to Jerusalem at the great festivals. You must keep the Sabbath holy and go to the synagogue to learn from the religious leaders. And you must study the law of God and obey it meticulously. Do, do, do!

Jesus changed all that. He drove the moneychangers out of the temple and told the religious leaders that One greater than the temple was among them. He repeatedly healed people on the Sabbath day, so as to demonstrate that He was in charge of the Sabbath, not vice versa. And He gave His followers a new law—to love one another as He had loved them. Revolutionary stuff, and in the end it goaded the religious authorities to hound Him to death. He had set Himself up against the whole religious establishment!

—*Who Is This Jesus?*, MICHAEL GREEN

When Jesus came to our world, he did not introduce another religion. The world to which he came did not need another religion. Religion had become the problem, not the answer! *Bad News Religion* still is the problem! Authentic, grace-based Christianity was the answer Jesus gave us, not another system of things to do, rituals to complete, spiritual obstacle courses to conquer and religious credentials to be earned.

Paul graphically explained that all the religious credentials he had accumulated before Jesus appeared to him on the road to Damascus amounted to one big pile of rubbish (Philippians 3:8). Legalism becomes a continuous push to do-do-do resulting in a giant pile of rubbish.

Christ came as our High Priest. He, once and for all, took care of our sin problem. Once and for all he defeated death and the grave. He died and rose again so that we too may have the same victory, and that's the only way we will have this victory.

There isn't enough time in all the days of our lives to build enough character, to do enough good, or to perform enough righteous deeds to earn our own victory.

Victory is ours by God's grace alone. God doesn't need, nor does he ask for, our help in this task. Jesus Christ has already finished that work. Salvation is by God's grace alone. God gives us his grace because of the work Jesus did, and grace is all we need. It is sufficient!

OUR HIGH PRIEST SAT DOWN!

Hebrews was written at a time when the temple in Jerusalem was still standing, and when the Old Covenant priesthood was still in full operation. Contrasting the work of Christ, our High Priest, with the work of the priests of the Old Covenant, Hebrews tells us,

> Day after day every priest *stands* and *performs* his religious duties; again and again he offers the same sacrifices, which can never take away sins. But when this priest had offered for all time one sacrifice for sins, he *sat down* at the right hand of God.
>
> —HEBREWS 10:11–12 *(emphasis added)*

When Jesus sat down, he made history. No priest had ever been able to sit down before. There was always something to be done. The work was never finished. But when Jesus came as our High Priest he finished all the work. He completed all the work that needed to be done. His last statement from the cross was "It is finished" (John 19:30). It's over, once and for all!

The cross of Christ reminds us of God's love for us, and the victory he achieved that we can never achieve on our own, but by God's grace, we can receive. The empty tomb reminds us that Christ is not there anymore, but that he is risen, he is alive, he has conquered all religion—and he lives to give us freedom from the deadly virus of legalism.

A healthy, grace-based church will emphasize the work of Christ. He alone has brought about our salvation; and when he was finished, he sat down. It is finished.

Chapter Five—Review and Recap

Getting older. The mere process of aging can help bring God's amazing grace into focus.

Keeping up appearances. *Bad News Religion* leads us to focus on appearances—the external trappings, rituals, issues, and activities of religion—rather than the invisible power of God's grace.

What we do versus what Christ did. *Bad News Religion* emphasizes the works and virtues we humans can produce. Authentic Christianity, by contrast, is all about what Jesus has done.

Externalism diminishes God's grace. Grace is the unseen power of God, and because it cannot be seen it is often devalued by those who place their trust and hope in the external trappings of religion.

No chair in the temple. The work of the priests of the Old Covenant was never done. The work of our High Priest is done. It is finished.

Old Covenant externals. The Old Covenant is an example of the futility of religion based on externals. It stands in stark contrast to the New Covenant, which is based on the inner working of God's grace.

6

Quid Pro Quo

"All the world religions can be placed in one of two camps: legalism or grace. Humankind does it or God does it. Salvation as a wage based on deeds alone—or salvation as a gift based on Christ's death."

—*He Still Moves Stones*, MAX LUCADO

ARE YOU WEARY AND SPIRITUALLY EXHAUSTED? Tired of feeling inadequate, believing that you don't measure up, that you aren't good enough? Do you feel that *Bad News Religion* has spiritually mugged you, and left you by the side of the road (Luke 10:30)? Let me share some life-changing news with you— some news that might even seem too good to be true! Let's start with this passage from Ephesians 2:

> But because of his great love for us, God, who is rich in mercy, made us alive with Christ even when we were dead in transgressions—it is by grace you have been saved. And God raised us up with Christ and seated us with him in the heavenly realms in Christ Jesus, in order that in the coming ages he might show the incomparable riches of his grace, expressed in his kindness to us in Christ Jesus. For it is by grace you have been saved, through faith—and this not

from yourselves—it is the gift of God—not by works, so that no one can boast. For we are God's workmanship, created in Christ Jesus to do good works, which God prepared in advance for us to do.

—EPHESIANS 2:4–10

The subject of this passage is God's grace, and what it means to us. Here are eight definitions of grace, this profoundly beautiful and liberating word:

1. God's goodness and generosity.

2. A free gift, with "no strings attached."

3. A free gift of such magnitude that no repayment is possible, let alone required.

4. A free gift of such value that only God can give, and that no human can ever earn or acquire by effort or merit.

5. A state of sanctification—a spiritual reality and environment in which God's children live.

6. Kindness, mercy and clemency—a reprieve and pardon.

7. Approval and favor.

8. The nature, essence, character and economy of God.

Let's also consider a negative definition. What is the very opposite of grace? Notice the last definition in the list above. "The nature, essence, character, and economy of God." What's the opposite of that? In short, the way we humans are. Our nature, essence, character, and economy are all about vanity, jealousy, lust, and greed. Get, take, possess, fight, quarrel, bicker, covet, and envy. The way we operate and deal with each other can be summed up by the Latin phrase, *quid pro quo.*

Quid Pro Quo = Something for Something

Quid pro quo means "something for something—something received or given in return for something else." We humans learn quickly that we must work for what we get in our world. We earn wages for services we render. *Quid pro quo.* We earn approval and acceptance by deeds we perform. *Quid pro quo.* People like and love us if we help them, serve them, and make them feel or look good. *Quid pro quo.*

Grace is the opposite of *quid pro quo.* God is grace. He gives and loves, without guarantee or prior evidence of any return on his investment. Not only does God not reward us for what we deserve, he gives us what we can never deserve. God returns good for evil, because when all is said and done, the best we humans can ever accomplish is tainted by sin. The product of our lives is at best flawed and imperfect. But God is grace—he does not respond to us "in kind"—he does not respond on a *quid pro quo* basis—but instead he returns good for evil. God is grace.

Do you understand? I don't—not completely. On this issue, and many other spiritual realities, because we are physical, mortal, limited human beings we can only "see but a poor reflection as in a mirror" (1 Corinthians 13:12). But grace is the good news of the gospel, it is the anchor of our spiritual lives in Christ; it is the bedrock of Christian faith. While we may not *comprehend* grace completely during our earthly sojourn on this side of eternity, because of Jesus we may *apprehend* it by accepting and receiving it.

The very fact that grace is so unlike the way we humans operate and deal with each other—the very fact that grace seems "too good to be true"—is the primary reason why humans often do not accept this wonderful gift God offers to us all. We simply cannot believe it, for no one has ever related to us on that basis before—why, we reason, should God?

I like the crisp definition of grace offered by Frederick Buechner in his book, *Wishful Thinking* (cited at the beginning of the fifth chapter). He explains that it all comes down to the sentence, "There's nothing you have to do"—and he explains that it helps to place emphasis on three different words in that sentence, *you*, *have*, and *do*. "There's nothing *you* have to do. There's nothing you *have* to do. There's nothing you have to *do*."

> **Not only does God not reward us for what we deserve, he gives us what we can never deserve.**

Earlier, I called attention to the fact that there was one piece of furniture "missing" in the tabernacle and temple. No chair. No place to sit down. The lesson is obvious. The work of the priests of Israel was never done. The priests never had enough time to offer enough sacrifices to make the nation of Israel righteous. And if somehow they would have been able to find enough time, there were not enough animals to sacrifice to atone for the sins of Israel.

But Christ came as our High Priest. He defeated the spurious claims and demands of religion. He died and rose again so that we too may have the same victory. There is not enough time in the days of our lives to do enough good or perform enough righteous deeds, rituals or sacrifices so that we can earn our own victory.

Remember, there were no chairs, and certainly no recliners or rocking chairs, in the tabernacle or temple because there was always something to be finished. The work was never done. But when Jesus came as our High Priest he finished all the work of salvation. He completed all the work that needed to be done.

That's good news! But it gets better! Remember the passage we read, at the beginning of this chapter, from Ephesians 2:4–10? Let's notice verse six again:

> And God raised us up with Christ and *seated us* with him in
> the heavenly realms in Christ Jesus.
> —EPHESIANS 2:6 *(emphasis added)*

Note the verb tense. The book of Ephesians, written almost 2,000 years ago, says that Christians are now seated with Christ. The Bible says nothing about your seat being reserved for you *pending* your good works. The Bible says that those who accept Jesus Christ are seated—*right now*—no reservation needed and no waiting.

In the name of Christ, religious counterfeits require that we give a bribe or tip to the headwaiter to get into the dining area. Performance-based religion gives preference to who and what you know, how much you have and what you have accomplished. But Jesus offers everyone a seat in the most exclusive dining room in the universe, in the heavenly realms, based upon God's grace. Our seat at the Lord's Table is not based upon money, fame, or deeds. We are seated at the Lord's Table because of who he is, not because of who we are. And, by the way, the Bible says nothing about any particular group of believers being given preferential seating!

Bad News Religion not only convinces us that we may not sit down at the Lord's table, but it lies to us, persuading us that our services are required in God's spiritual kitchen. It insists that we perform like a frenzied short-order cook, frantically mixing, blending, frying, baking, and broiling. Performance-based religion not only mandates that we have a hand in producing our own spiritual food, but it gives us strict lists and recipes that we must follow. It assures us that our compliance to its prescriptions, formulas, and cookbooks will enable us to help manufacture our own salvation. Religious ingredients vary, but they always focus on how often and how much we must do specific things.

But God has neither assigned us to the kitchen nor invited us to help prepare our spiritual feast. Our place is sitting down at the Lord's Table, not stewing in the kitchen. God has a different way to produce what he wants us to become. He tells us that Jesus is the Master Chef, and there is room for only one cook in God's kitchen.

Performance-based religion is based on do-do-do. Obsessive rule keeping does not offer rest in Christ in its bag of tricks. It demands that we stand, hop, jump, and run, and that we dance to its tune.

What We Must Do

We must accept the offer to sit down. Christ will not *make* us sit down. He will not force us to accept his grace. Grace is ours only if we will reach out and accept the outstretched hand of our Lord and Savior. The seat that Jesus offers you is freedom from the oppression of trying to work your way into God's good graces and never being good enough.

Why don't more people sit down with Christ? If we accept Christ's gift of being seated with him in heavenly realms, we have to admit that we are powerless to perform enough good deeds to get ourselves into God's good graces. It is humbling to accept God's grace—because we would rather try to "do it" ourselves.

Do you remember what happened when Jesus visited the home of Martha and Mary? "Martha was distracted by all the preparations that had to be made" (Luke 10:40). But Mary "sat at the Lord's feet listening to what he said" (v. 39). Martha even became angry with her sister Mary, because she was sitting down. Those who trust in Christ and accept God's grace can actually make others angry— even their own families! God's grace angers legalism and the people it affects, infects, and controls.

Generally, the people who become most angry with God's children who sit down to listen to Jesus are people who are busy doing what they think will make God happy. Performance-based religion keeps us busy doing, performing, and accomplishing religious duties and obligations. Legalism keeps us busy because it doesn't really want us to listen, ponder, and consider the words of Jesus. We are expected to work harder and do more, so that all the right things are said and done. We become trapped in an endless cycle of activity.

Authentic Christians, are, of course, servants. If Jesus lives his life in us we will serve others, offering our time, talents, and treasures as spiritual acts of worship (Romans 12:1). But religious legalism can counterfeit Christ-centered service, sabotaging what Jesus does in and through us, convincing us that the things we do are obligating God to reward us. Legalism can persuade us what we have produced by God's grace is our hard work, not Jesus who works in us, and consequently hardworking people can become deeply offended when they see others resting in God's grace.

Consider the parable of the workers in the vineyard (Matthew 20:1–16). It's a story about God's grace, and how we react to it. The owner/employer is the central figure in this drama, in control of the harvest from the beginning of the parable to the end. The owner/employer of the vineyard is trying to harvest all of his grapes in one day. The grape harvest in Israel is in the early fall, with the work day at that time being from about 6 a.m. to 6 p.m. Farm workers who worked for him all year long went to the vineyard while the owner went to the marketplace to look for day workers.

He went to where day laborers congregated looking for work. We can see such places today in most North American cities. If you watch the action long enough at these informal gathering places, you will see potential employers drive up, discuss a job and a price, and often a number of workers will hop in the vehicle to go to the job site. Day laborers don't have a steady job or one employer on whom they can depend, so the offer of work is itself a gift.

You may know the story of the parable. The owner of the vineyard wants to harvest all of the grapes in one day, and the initial groups of day laborers he hires are not sufficient to get the job done in the time available. The owner makes several trips back to the marketplace to hire more help.

As the owner of the vineyard continues to hire more groups of workers, the day progresses, and the workers who have previously been hired, along with those who work for him all the time, continue to labor in the field. As the day goes by the owner becomes convinced that the job is not going to get done on time, so he makes more trips to the labor exchange, hiring workers who have simply been passing the time of day until he hires them.

Finally, he makes one more trip for more help. It's 5:00 p.m. Only one more hour of work left. Again, he hires more workers.

Hebrew law demanded that workers be paid at the end of the day (see Leviticus 19:13 and Deuteronomy 24:15). So the owner instructs that a paymaster dispense the wages, but he wants those who have worked the least time to be paid first while those who have worked longest, and presumably hardest, to wait to be paid until all others have received their wages.

Now we come to the moral of the story, and why all of this background is provided. Jesus is now going to help us understand more about God and his amazing grace, as well as provide some insight into human responses to God's grace.

When the workers who have worked but a short time are paid one denarius, they are elated. One denarius was the normal, expected wage for a full day's work. They might have expected that their pay would have been adjusted according to the exact time they worked. But instead, they received a fair wage for an entire day's work, even though they had not worked the entire day. They knew they were receiving God's grace and did not have to be convinced that they received more than they earned.

The owner, in stipulating that the last hired be paid first, must have wanted those who worked longest and hardest to see what he would pay the others. Had he done things differently, those who worked through the heat of the day would have taken their pay and gone home. But the owner of the vineyard wanted them to not only *experience* his grace, but to *observe* his grace at work in the lives of others.

The Bible says that those who worked the entire day, upon seeing those who only worked a few hours receive a denarius, assumed that they would receive more than the normal pay. Their expectations dimmed, however, as the pay remained the same for all those in line, regardless of the efforts and work they had expended.

Finally, those who worked the entire day received their pay. One denarius. Just like those who had not worked as hard, or as long! You can imagine the scene. They complained bitterly.

> These men who were hired last worked only one hour...and you have made them equal to us who have borne the burden of the work and the heat of the day.
>
> —MATTHEW 20:12

The landowner explained to this group of workers that he was not being unfair to them. They received the expected wage. He told them that he didn't do anything hurtful or grievous to them. The owner of the vineyard then declared that he had the right to do what he wanted with his money. And, while he didn't state it, it is obvious that he could easily have economized and saved money by not being so generous with the other workers. Then the landowner, still apparently seeing some major grievances being displayed, addressed the bottom line:

> Or are you envious because I am generous?
>
> —MATTHEW 20:15

Here comes the big hurt. The owner/employer has demonstrated goodness, generosity, and grace, while these workers are responding with greed and envy. Their real issue is not with how the owner of the vineyard treated them, but how much better he treated others who, in their estimation, did not deserve the same pay. They were upset because of what they perceived as a lack of equity and fairness.

Our world, our culture, and our economy work on the principle of barter. I work for you, and you pay me a fair wage. *Quid pro quo.* The harder I work, the longer I work, the more I believe I should earn. But God persistently tells us that the kingdom of heaven does not work on that earthbound principle. Effort, merit, and ability are not factored into grace. God gives his grace when, how, and to whom he wishes. And, more than that, God gives and dispenses grace, not favor based on our performance.

God is the owner of the vineyard. He does not calculate wages, nor does he compute his own "profit" by our rules, regulations, or expectations. God is not good to us because we have been good to him. God is good to us because he is good. His goodness does not depend on us. He owns the vineyard, he is in charge, and his finances are unlimited. He lavishly doles out the riches of his grace—completely undeserved, more-than-fair gifts without regard to our merit or hard work.

God does not help those who help themselves because they have worked hard to do what they should. God does not respond to us or "pay" us according to some exact percentage calculated from the precise number of good works that we perform. God wants us to know that we do not deserve what we work for in his vineyard, because there is no way that our efforts can ever earn what he freely gives us.

We do not receive God's grace based on a meticulous calculation of our efforts. God does not increase his grace if we attend church twice a week or every day, compared to someone who attends once a week, once a month or once a year. How often we attend or that we attend at all has no merit in our standing with God. Our deeds have no bearing on an increase in God's lavish and liberal dispensing of his grace. No one deserves God's grace, no matter how long we work in his vineyard, no matter how hot it gets when we work or how tired we might be when payday comes.

The work in the parable of the laborers in the vineyard has no direct bearing on God's grace. No *quid pro quo*. The opportunity to work in God's vineyard is itself a gift. Christ calls us to his rest, the rest that we can have in him, rest from the guilt and bondage of worrying whether we will be able to work hard enough to "make it," "get into heaven" or whether we can ever do enough to convince God to save us. God has saved us, because of and by his grace.

What do we *have to do?* All we "have to do" is surrender, swallow our pride, admit that the most virtuous deeds we have ever performed have nothing to do with God's grace, and accept Jesus Christ as our Lord and Savior. Any service we perform should be a response to grace, not for the purpose of accumulating points to earn God's favor.

The parable of the laborers in the vineyard also teaches us to be delighted when we see others receiving his grace, whether we think they have jumped through enough religious hoops or not. We may not feel that others upon whom God showers his grace have paid their dues, but God is not interested in any dues that humans are capable of paying. His grace is sufficient. All we need is grace.

Jesus calls on us to give up the futility of thinking that we must, or can, earn his good graces. He says:

> Come to *me*, all you who are weary and burdened, and I will give you rest. Take my yoke upon you and learn from *me*, for I am gentle and humble in heart, and you will find rest for your souls. For *my* yoke is easy and *my* burden is light.
>
> —MATTHEW 11:28–30 *(emphasis added)*

DO YOU REALLY WANT WHAT YOU DESERVE?

You have probably heard about the eye for an eye principle of justice. An eye for an eye was a fundamental basis of retributive justice under the Old Covenant. You may have also heard the astute observation that an eye for an eye will eventually leave everyone blind.

In his Sermon on the Mount (Matthew 5–7) Jesus directly confronted and challenged the implications and teachings of the Old Covenant. He actually points out that the demands of the law are much greater than anyone could satisfy. The Sermon on the Mount is a radical imperative warning that the birth, life, death, and resurrection of Jesus would forever change, revolutionize, and transform religion. In these three critically important chapters of Matthew, Jesus is telling us that he has come as life and light to a world of legalistic religion.

The Sermon on the Mount eliminates religion as a "middle-man" between God and us. The Sermon on the Mount is a message that Jesus changes everything. The New Covenant is all about him. The New Covenant is all about God's grace.

> You have heard that it was said, "Eye for eye, and tooth for tooth." But I tell you, do not resist an evil person. If some-one strikes you on the right cheek, turn to him the other also. And if someone wants to sue you and take your tunic, let him have your cloak as well. If someone forces you to go one mile, go with him two miles. Give to the one who asks you, and do not turn away from the one who wants to bor-row from you.
>
> —MATTHEW 5:38–42

Retributive justice requires a direct connection between the crime and the punishment. The crime and the pain inflicted must be returned to the one who is deemed to have initially caused it. The closer and more exacting the punishment fits the crime, the more sense of closure humans tends to have. We believe that retributive justice is fair because the punishment fits the crime.

There are many on-going feuds, battles, and wars in our world that are nothing more than an attempt to ensure that justice is done via the eye for an eye principle. A literal and strict application of this principle often amounts to nothing more than escalating violence, as each party attempts to vindicate itself and its cause as it responds to strikes and counterstrikes.

Consider the conflict in the Middle East between Jews and Arabs. I have traveled to Israel and Jordan several times, attempting to understand this unholy deadlock. Israelis have often told me, "You can't make peace with the Arabs." Amazingly, I have received the same comment from Palestinians, "You can't make peace with the Jews."

The Jews and Palestinians are locked into a vicious cycle of violence. Both sides seek revenge—the eye for an eye desire to see the other side suffer because of the pain and misery they have directly or indirectly caused over the centuries. Both sides are keeping score, with the grim justice of an eye for an eye and a tooth for a tooth driving action and reaction.

An eye for an eye can encourage us to focus on the inadequacies and shortcomings of others. Retributive justice can become a matter of denying personal responsibility while attributing blame for our actions to others. It's much like the arguments that little children have when parents intervene in their fighting and quarreling. "He started it" is the normal human justification and reaction.

Jesus comes into our world of recrimination and revenge proclaiming grace that will end human squabbles and bickering. He tells us that it doesn't matter who started the fight or battle. He tells us that any idea of ensuring that the bad guys get what is coming to them is based in our worldly kingdoms, not in the kingdom of heaven. The kingdom of heaven proclaims an end to revenge, insults, atrocities, and hostilities in the name of "an eye for an eye." Strikes and counterstrikes end with the kingdom of heaven.

When God, in the person of Jesus, came into our world, he embodied grace. God entered the human story being played out on the stage of planet earth, having already written himself into our story as the Lamb slain from the creation of the world (Revelation 13:8). Jesus inserted himself into our story and told us that the focus of our lives is not all about getting what we deserve.

Grace is not an eye for an eye, but going the extra mile, turning the other cheek, giving our coat to someone in need. God empowers us, as his children, to respond to negativity, insults, and hostility with grace. Even though our humanity cries out for its definition of justice and a fair shake, even though we hunger to see the other guy get what's coming to him, Jesus calls us to the higher path of grace. For Jesus, the sinner is not a candidate for punishment or execution, but the sinner is a candidate for redemption. The grace of God is not about what we or someone else deserve. After all, do we really want what we deserve?

TWO WAYS OF BEING JUDGED

The Bible tells us that we have two ways of being judged, and the choice is ours. We may be judged on the basis of what we have produced, or we may be judged on the basis of what Christ produced. We can choose: 1) our works or 2) the works of Christ. We can ask God to give us salvation, or deny it, on the basis of what we deserve—or we can throw ourselves on God's mercy and appeal to his grace because of what Christ did for us.

Grace is the very opposite of getting what we deserve. Performance-based religion is the idea that we work for and earn our rewards—when we get what we deserve. The gospel of Jesus Christ teaches us that what we deserve is death.

> For the wages of sin is death, but the gift of God is eternal life in Christ Jesus our Lord.
>
> —ROMANS 6:23

What we deserve, what we earn—our paycheck—is death. That's the only logical end to our lives because we have all sinned and find ourselves unable to pay the debt of our sin by our own efforts. A lifetime of obedience, of good works, of perfect church attendance, of formal prayer three or more times a day, of feeding the poor or evangelizing the lost—or of any other beneficial, moral, and ethical action—will not erase our sin and earn us a ticket into God's kingdom of heaven.

That fact, of course, has not stopped tens of millions of sincere men and women who are urged by legalism to insist on paying their own way and purchasing their own ticket to the kingdom of heaven. Humanly, we would attempt to do it ourselves, rather than accept God's grace. And religious legalism capitalizes on our pride. We don't like handouts.

Legalism seduces us by promising us that we can earn our own way into God's good graces. Performance-based religion is a harsh and stern slave driver. Religious externalism leads tens of millions into the swamp of despair and frustration where they are doomed to a lifetime of endless toil trying to please and appease the gods of religion.

Isn't it ironic that legalism threatens humans with hell if they don't measure up and perform, but in reality the hell it threatens is the hell it produces in the lives of its slaves? Many live wretched lives in the hellish swamps of legalism, trapped by an obsession with good deeds they attempt to produce, threatened with continuing and intensified hell in the afterlife. Apart from Christ we cannot be freed. I know, for I have been to religious hell and by God's grace returned to tell you this story.

I know many "good" and sincere people, many of them dear friends, who are deceived by the premise that what they are doing is making God happy. They absolutely believe that what they do has some impact upon their salvation, and that in the end God will reward them for the unique and sometimes bizarre things they do and believe.

These people are absolutely convinced that their beliefs and behaviors distinguish them as God's one and only, true, special people. They believe that in the end God will be obligated to reward them because they have earned it, fair and square.

We find it hard to accept the outstretched hand of our Savior. It's difficult to accept God's grace—especially if grace has been demonized by the particular name brand of legalism that has bewitched and brainwashed us. It is excruciating to face the truth that we cannot deserve anything other than death for all of our works.

So, do we really want what we deserve? Do we want to try to work out the bill for our salvation on our terms? Do we understand the enormity of the bill, as we reach for the check, insisting that God allow us to pay for our own salvation? Do we actually think that we can earn God's favor? We do, if we listen to the pied pipers of *Bad News Religion,* and their voices are everywhere around us, including many who beckon to us in the name of Jesus Christ.

Paul tells us in Romans 6:23 that our paycheck for everything that we do, good and bad, is death. But in the same breath, in the same verse, he tells us that the good news is that eternal life is free of charge. Thank God that eternal life in God's kingdom of heaven is not based upon what you and I deserve, but upon God's magnificent and matchless grace.

Thank God that he has made a way to spare us a life and an eternity of fairness. We do not get what we deserve in this life, no matter how hard we try to ensure that we do. Not getting what we deserve means that there are times when we suffer loss and receive injustice. But the rest of the story is that God offers us his grace. God's grace is something else that we do not deserve. If we accept God's grace, the times in our physical lives when we do not receive what we consider to be justice pale by comparison when we realize that God forgives us of the many things we do deserve.

Not getting what we deserve is, in the end, far better than receiving everything we do deserve. That's why John Newton, the former slave ship captain, called it *Amazing Grace.*

CHAPTER SIX—REVIEW AND RECAP

Something for something. Human beings operate according to the principle of *quid pro quo*—something received in return for something else.

Works for rewards. *Bad News Religion* also operates on the principle of *quid pro quo*— if we give God our good deeds and obedience, legalistic religion promises that God will give us his favor.

Grace. God's grace is the opposite of *quid pro quo*. He freely gives, in spite of what we have or haven't done.

Grace for nothing. The parable of the workers in the vineyard teaches us that God does not pay us according to what we do or what we deserve. We can do nothing to earn what God gives us.

God's grace given because he is generous. God gives and dispenses grace based solely upon his generosity. His favor is not gained by our performance.

Our work or his? We can choose to be judged on the basis of what we have produced, or we can choose to be judged on the basis of what Christ has produced.

An example for us. God's grace encourages us to behave graciously. Grace is not an eye for an eye, but is rather turning the other cheek, going the extra mile, and giving our coat to someone in need.

7

Legalism Strikes Back!

*"But what has been the result? A Christianity that is itself a religion. . . .
A religion marked by all the traits of religion: myths, legends, rites, holy
things, beliefs, clergy, etc. A Christianity that has fashioned a morality—
and what a morality!—the most strict, the most moralistic, the most
debilitating, the one that reduces adherents to infants and renders them
irresponsible, or if I were to be malicious, I should say the one that makes
of them happy imbeciles, who are sure of their salvation if they obey this
morality. . . ."*

—*The Subversion of Christianity,* Jacques Ellul

*"Christians are still angry at the world for being so bad, and the world is
angry at Christians for thinking Christians are so good. . . . Of course
God doesn't hate the world; we hate the world. And we like to think that
God agrees with us, that God is on our side."*

—*Fearless Faith,* John Fischer

I WAS ONCE A GUEST SPEAKER at a church, and as the pastor
and I drove to church he told me that we were a little ahead of
time. He asked me if he could show me something. We stopped
at a McDonald's a few miles from his church. We ordered coffee and
within a few seconds the pastor was surrounded by senior citizens
who were having breakfast with Ronald McDonald.

Later, in the car, I asked the pastor about those people. "Those
are my friends, people I am reaching out to. They do not trust their

church anymore. They don't believe their church cares for them. They are upset about the sacrifices they made for their church, and all of the work they did, but now their church doesn't seem to care."

The pastor explained to me that these people were so turned off from the demands of their church that they wanted nothing to do with Christianity. He had slowly befriended them, visited them, and prayed with and for them. But, he said, "I don't know if some of these wonderful people will ever darken the door of any church again. They need help, they need spiritual direction and nourishment, so I meet them where they are—at McDonalds."

> **There is no ritual, no deed, no church tradition, no human innovation, nor any ceremony that imparts grace. Grace comes from God and God alone.**

There are people who will never come back to *any* church because of *the* church. What have we done? And more to the point, what are we doing, or not doing?

Jesus once healed a man who had been blind from birth (John 9:25). Not only did he heal the man, but he did it on the Sabbath— a direct challenge to religious restrictions adopted by Judaism. Of course, this healing was not simply the restoration of sight—this miracle of God's grace involved the gift of sight this man never had.

The reaction of the Pharisees was predictable. Jesus was a threat. He healed—and he did it in spite of and in the face of their religion. The Bible doesn't tell us about any party the Pharisees threw for the man, or any flowers they delivered to his house. Not only did the Pharisees forget to mail invitations to the party, but their reaction to

God's grace was to have an investigation (would that be anything like an inquisition?)

The Pharisees were angry. They tried to deny and revise what actually had happened. They denied that the man ever had been blind to begin with. They questioned whether anyone who did not jump through the same religious hoops as they did could do any good. For their religion to stand this challenge the Pharisees would have to discredit Jesus and deny the truth of what had happened. After all, they knew that this miracle had taken place in spite of their religion, not because of it.

The first explanation they could offer was that this was not the man who everyone knew as a blind man, rather it was simply someone who looked like him. But, the formerly blind man insisted that he had actually been healed.

The Pharisees then used another popular legalistic technique to persuade and convince—they tried to bully and intimidate the man. When the man said that Jesus was a prophet, and that he healed him, the Pharisees intensified the pressure. While they continued to cross-examine the man who had been healed, they questioned the man's parents to see if they could be pressured into saying that there was some other explanation for this healing other than God's grace.

> The Jews still did not believe that he had been blind and had received his sight until they sent for the man's parents. "Is this your son?" they asked. "Is this the one you say was born blind? How is it that now he can see?" "We know he is our son," the parents answered, "and we know he was born blind. But how he can see now, or who opened his eyes, we don't know. Ask him. He is of age; he will speak for himself." His parents said this because they were afraid of the Jews,

for already the Jews had decided that anyone who acknowledged that Jesus was the Christ would be put out of the synagogue. That was why his parents said, "He is of age, ask him."

—JOHN 9:18–23

Bad News Religion strikes back when grace is given. Religious legalism, by definition, is not gracious. There is no ritual, no deed, no church tradition, no human innovation, nor any ceremony that imparts grace. Grace comes from God and from God alone. Grace is a direct challenge to legalism's authority. There is only one response that religion based on externalism can give—and only one response that externalism has ever given to grace—anger, hatred, and animosity.

WARRING AGAINST GRACE

Legalism is at war with grace, because grace will put *Bad News Religion* out of business. Religion realized that Jesus was a threat to its business when he came as Immanuel, God with us. Performance-based religion has opposed the gospel of Jesus Christ from the beginning, doing its best to twist, pervert, and corrupt authentic Christianity.

This tunnel vision convinces some Christians to condemn and target so-called mortal enemies of Christianity. And then after all of the vilification and invective, Christians wonder why non-Christians don't start coming to church. Why wouldn't more people accept an invitation to be mugged and beaten up?

Some Christians boycott, protest, condemn, and fulminate that the world is going to hell in a handbasket. Meanwhile, back at the ranch, authentic Christianity is under attack. As a result much of

Christendom is in danger of capitulation, largely due to its state of ungrace and the negative fruit produced by *Bad News Religion.*

The deadly virus of religious legalism within churches convinces churchgoers that they are better than others, and that it is their job to confront people to "wake them up." This deadly virus is corrupting the gospel, making its message seem irrelevant, and obsolete. Performance-based religion is attempting to suffocate and choke authentic Christianity. The love of God is being replaced by the fear and hate of externalism.

There are many who call themselves Christians who are angry with the world Jesus loves. When the World Trade Center and Pentagon were bombed on September 11, 2001, some Christians said that God was angry at the United States because of our sins and that he was punishing us. While there is no doubt that God judged the nation of Israel in the Old Testament, it is a giant leap to attribute all disasters, diseases, and destruction as God's direct punishment.

Somewhere along the line some who call themselves Christians have gotten the idea that God wants Christians to criticize, condemn, intimidate, and bully other people. I have searched the Bible, to no avail, to find teaching that would direct me to boycott and wave placards. I have searched the history of the early church in an effort to see how those who were eyewitnesses of Jesus' life and ministry might have engaged in such things.

Nothing.

Where do we get such ideas? Not from the Bible. Where then? We get these ideas from *Bad News Religion,* the mortal enemy of God's grace.

We, in our flesh, get angry when God bestows his grace without measure. When God spends some of the riches of his grace to throw a lavish and expensive party to welcome the prodigal son home, obsessive rule keepers do not even come to the party. When Jesus gave sight to a man who had been born blind, religious externalism was not happy. It is our nature to become upset when someone who does not work as hard or as long as we do and still gets the same gift. We are troubled when someone is sitting down, resting in Christ, instead of knocking themselves out with rules and rituals.

Religious legalism loses its cool when those who follow Jesus don't rush around doing all the "right" things. It operates on the eye for an eye principle and can only see grace as weak and useless.

Here's what the Bible says. Jesus told us that we can know his disciples by the love he gives them and by the fact that his love will be reflected in their lives (John 13:35). Authentic Christians have peace and joy—they are kind and patient (Galatians 5:22–23). There is nothing at all about threats and intimidation.

The Hotter the Better

Within Christendom legalism exerts pressure for a belief in and proclamation of the hottest kind of hell. There is a kind of theological one-upmanship with which performance-based religion has infected some congregations and denominations. This belief seems to boil down to the idea that the more faithful and diligent a Christian you are the hotter the hell in which you believe. *Bad News Religion* causes people to boast that they are better than others because their hell is hotter.

I believe in hell, in spite of the bizarre and unbiblical ideas about hell that some within Christendom insist on. I believe that hell is eternal separation from God—the very opposite of heaven, which is eternity spent in God's presence.

I believe in hell because I believe what the Bible teaches about good and evil, about the grace of God and the judgment of God. But I do not believe that people who avoid playing cards, seeing a movie, or drinking the beverage that Jesus created in his first miracle auto-matically earn a "get out of hell free" card. There's *Bad News Religion* again. Do stuff and stay out of hell. That's the legalism of religion that is the polar opposite of God's grace.

Legalism says that if we obey a rule we win a prize. In some people's books staying out of hell is all about what you do, as defined by a narrow and restrictive religious system of dos and don'ts. God's grace says that we are given his grace because he loves us. The truth is that we stay out of hell because of God's grace.

You may have heard about the religious man who used to lie awake at night unable to sleep because he was convinced that some-where someone was getting away with something. This is the kind of person that performance based religion can turn us into.

The Bible does not give Christians a mandate to be judge, jury, and executioner of those who come short of perfection. The Bible directs followers of Jesus Christ to love and forgive, not to criticize and condemn. The Bible gives Christians no authority to "scare the hell" out of people in the interests of getting them into heaven or keeping them out of hell.

Bad News Religion spares no effort in its attempt to convince its followers that all people outside of its rules and traditions will suffer an awful fate. It leads to arrogance and high-handed, holier than thou attitudes, ridiculing, maligning, and making fun of those who are outside of the boundaries.

Many North Americans believe in a stereotype of Christianity that presents Christians as mad, angry, bitter, and filled with con-demnation. Non-Christians see Christians as confrontational and holier-than-thou. Those who do not even pretend to follow Jesus Christ often define Christians not by what we stand for but by what we stand against.

I've had people tell me that they wouldn't mind being a

Christian if they didn't have to become religious in the process. Think about that. The gospel of Jesus Christ calls us out of legalism, but unfortunately the message that some preach in his name is that you have to be infected by legalism in order to be a Christian!

The good news of God's grace is that you *can* follow Jesus without becoming a slave of *Bad News Religion.*

THE PAGAN GODS OF COUNTERFEIT CHRISTIANITY

Christianity is *monotheistic*—worshiping one God. It shares this belief with Islam and Judaism, but Christianity is unique in its acceptance of the biblical revelation that God is one, yet he is Father, Son, and Holy Spirit. The Trinity is the most foundational of all Christian doctrines. Virtually all heretical and much abusive teaching that departs from authentic Christian teaching (orthodoxy) and practice (orthopraxis) can be traced back to a fundamental misunderstanding of the nature of God. How can authentic Christianity be based on a relationship with God if we do not know or understand the God of the Bible?

The Roman, Babylonian, and Greek pagan cultures were polytheistic; they did not worship the one true God, but instead created a pantheon of gods. Either in official doctrine or in practice, or both, polytheism is one of the basic building blocks of religion.

Polytheism (worship of many gods) has long been a descriptive definition of paganism. Not only is polytheism a radical departure from the one true God of the Bible; it works hand in glove with performance-based religion.

Worshipping many different gods of religion appeals to the human mind because we can deceive ourselves into thinking that ultimate power and control is not limited to the one true God. Religions that deny the one true God of the Bible often believe that ultimate power is shared by gods who have limited control over specific domains and spheres.

The lie of polytheism leads directly to the belief that our actions can influence God (or "the gods" in polytheistic terms) to conform to our desires. Paganism thus infiltrates Christianity via the avenue of performance and legalism. There are those who say they are Christians, and think that they are Christians, but their beliefs and practices identify them as nothing more than 21st century pagans.

Paganism has not only insinuated itself into our society but it has entered into many of our churches—threatening to turn those who think they are Christians into neo-pagans. Today, neo-paganism is thriving within Christendom via a "genie in a bottle god" that is presented to us as someone we can manipulate into performing miracles for us. This idea is attractive to us because it offers a god in a bottle, a god under our control, whom we can release from the bottle when we need him, but then after the crisis has passed we can put the god back in the bottle.

People have the illusion that they are in charge of their lives— they are sitting at the control panel of their own lives and can bargain and negotiate with God on the basis of their efforts and good deeds. The biblical truth of authentic Christianity is that the one true God is sovereign, almighty, and in charge of the universe.

Legalism offers a god whom we can control by our good works. Religion, often influenced by paganism, offers us the delusion that we have the power to determine our reward and our fate by the rituals and deeds we perform. While these ideas promote themselves in the name of Christ, at the end of the day they are nothing more than paganism. They are pagan because they misrepresent, distort, and pervert the relationship the one true God of the Bible offers us.

Bad News Religion offers us a Santa Claus god who will give us what we *want* if we are good. Instead, authentic Christianity tells us that God gives us what we *need* because *he* is good.

With the focus on what we do, paganism tells us that a god or the gods want us to do the best we can, and at the end he (or they) will judge us based upon our performance. Performance-based religion tells us that a Santa Claus god will let us into his heaven if we qualify, if we overcome and if we are good little boys and girls.

By promising us anything and everything *Bad News Religion* leads us to slavery, but never delivers. It's a carnival with many attractions—"something for everyone." The carnival of legalism offers booths where you can prove your spiritual strength, and in return you will be given a trinket or bauble that assures you that the gods are happy with you. The performance carnival presents attractions that promise physical healing and physical wealth, as long as you surrender your mind and your money. Positive thinking metaphysical magicians roam the Mardi Gras-like atmosphere, promising you that you can name and claim your every hope and dream.

Counterfeit Christianity does all of this and much more in the name of the God of the Bible, in the name of Jesus Christ, our Lord and Savior. Then, when people find out that they have been seduced and lied to, when the traveling circus and medicine show folds up its tents and leaves town, a trail of disappointment and bitterness is left in its wake.

When the one true God of the Bible, "I AM WHO I AM" (Exodus 3:14), encountered Moses he offered him freedom, but it was freedom on God's terms. This was no pagan god of polytheism that Moses could manipulate and manage. This was the one God, who the Bible teaches exists as three divine coeternal, coessential Persons—Father, Son and Holy Spirit. "I AM WHO I AM" is the one true God who redeems us from the sin of legalism—the idea that our deeds can manipulate him like a puppet.

This God of the Bible is the God of grace, not some false god whom religion portrays as a cosmic bell hop offering us room service, catering to our every whim and desire whenever we want it. The God of the Bible is not some god that humans have created in their own image. This is not some pagan god who promises to deliver the spiritual pizza we order to our home within 30 minutes of our order. This is the one true God who exists outside of the time-and-space world in which we live, who is the God of eternity past, present, and future. He always has been, is and always will be. He was, is and is to come (Revelation 1:4, 8; 4:8).

God came to Moses and told him to take off his shoes. God is in charge—God is setting the standards. God sets us free from the slavery we experience in our world, but he does so according to his conditions and provisions.

God promises to deliver us from the religion of Egypt—with all of its potions and magic, superstitions, illusions, magicians, and enticements. *Bad News Religion* bewitches, whether it is in Egypt, the Galatia to which Paul ministered (Galatians 3:1) or in our 21st century world. The authentic Christianity of the Bible sets us free from ignorance and from tyrannical religious Pharaohs.

The relationship the one true God of the Bible offers us is on his terms, by his grace, not because of any good thing we have done or ever can do. We are rescued, redeemed, and saved from the spiritual Egypts and mystery religions of our world when we surrender our desire to make God into our image, and ask him to be our Potter, yielding to him as his clay (Jeremiah 18:1–4; Romans 9:20–21).

CHAPTER SEVEN—REVIEW AND RECAP

Grace under attack. *Bad News Religion* will always attack grace, because grace is a threat to the religious status quo.

Human nature opposes grace. Like the older brother in the parable of the Prodigal Son, we can get angry when God lavishes his grace without measure.

Going to hell. *Bad News Religion* emphasizes condemnation and punishment. It controls people through fear by an overemphasis on hell. But Christians don't serve God out of fear of punishment. Christians obey God because of his grace and what he has done for us.

God in our pocket. Paganism claims that our actions can influence God and obligate him to give us our desires. Similar teachings have infiltrated Christendom in the name of Christ.

How God answers our prayers. God is not a cosmic bellhop who provides room service or delivers the spiritual pizza we order to our homes within 30 minutes.

8

Is the Good News "Easy Believism?"

"I must strive to love my sons unconditionally and to assure them of this love regardless of their behavior, for this is how God loves each one of us. Some Christians believe this is dangerous teaching. They are inclined to think that if people know God will love them even if they are bad, then nothing would motivate them to be good. However, this is faulty theology when placed beside the clear message of Scripture. It is not for us to decide the terms or conditions of God's love, and the Word of God clearly states that God loved us while we were yet sinners."

—*The Voice of Jesus,* Gordon T. Smith

THE PASTOR POUNDED THE PULPIT; "It's not a cake walk you know. Some of you think that all you have to do is accept Jesus, attend church when you feel like it, and give a few dollars in the offering basket. But you need to do more than that. Do you think Jesus died on the cross just so you can be a couch potato Christian?"

He paused, and surveyed the flock, before continuing, "And I hear that some of you are thinking of leaving our church to go to the big mega-church outside of town. You think that going to church in sloppy clothing, listening to rock music, and hearing a short message spiced up with footage from Holly-weird movies is better than coming to our church where you hear the old time gospel! You go right ahead and attend that church with its Las Vegas style productions, but let me warn you—that's nothing more than easy-believism. It isn't real Christianity. Christianity involves more than just entertainment."

The pastor is frustrated—he has lost several families to the mega-church, and he feels he has to protect his dwindling flock. The pastor isn't alone. A number of other small churches in town are feeling the pinch as members are being gobbled up by the big mega-church with its smiling, personable, tanned, joke-telling, casually dressed young pastor. The pastor and several of his fellow ministers are convinced that easy-believism is to blame.

In part, it is. Permissive churches entice us with ideas that we can do whatever we want to do whenever we want to do it, and in the American competitive religious market this means giving the people what they want. Authentic Christianity most certainly is not a case of a pastor determining what his people want and then getting out in front of them to lead them to their subjectively determined Promised Land.

There is no doubt that easy-believism is a major problem in the North American religious landscape. It is a heresy, a ditch into which many fall, an attractive alternative to authentic Christianity. It is the ditch of permissiveness and compromise. No question.

But there is an equal and opposite ditch, and legalism is its name. Legalism decries easy-believism, and rightly so. But in the process legalism often condemns God's amazing grace as well. Grace is so often characterized as permissiveness. There are pastors and ministry leaders who object to easy-believism on legalistic grounds—fearing that their big stick will be taken away from them, and they will no longer be able to control their congregations. We do have much to fear from easy-believism. We also have much to fear from legalistic religion. We have nothing to fear from God's grace.

One of the questions I hear most frequently goes something like this. "Okay. All you talk about is grace. So explain this. Since Christ's work on the cross is sufficient for my salvation, and since God loves me unconditionally, why should I even bother trying to obey him?"

It's a good question. Why try? Why obey? If it's all done for you, why be good? Is God's grace a license to sin? If God saves us by his grace, then why should we even try? The answer to this question lies at the heart of the amazing grace God offers to us.

God is more interested in our hearts than how well we cling to and comply with a set of rules and conditions. That's difficult for us to understand and accept. But whether we like it or not, Christianity is based on a relationship, not on rules. When human beings try to improve on Christianity and make it into a set of rules and regulations, legalism contaminates the authentic and pure gospel of Jesus Christ.

Let's clarify. By definition, Christians want to obey God. We want to make him happy. We want

Authentic Christianity most certainly is not a case of a pastor determining what his people want and then getting out in front of them to lead them to their subjectively determined Promised Land.

to do the things with which he'll be pleased. The Bible makes it clear that the children of God want to obey him, but that God's grace is the reason they want to obey him. Christians obey because they have been saved.

But why do we, and should we, strive to obey God if he's already saved us by grace? Jesus Christ did what he did without any guarantee that we would respond favorably. He loved us first, and we therefore love, honor, and desire to obey him.

When we are convicted that he has saved us, when we have accepted the outstretched hand of the Lord who is the Chief

Shepherd of our souls (see Psalm 23 and 1 Peter 2:25) we want to please him in every way. When we accept what Jesus Christ did for us, and trust in the love God has for us, we long to commit our lives to him. To deliberately turn our backs on him just because he says, "I've saved you by my grace not by what you do," and turn his grace into a license for sin (Galatians 5:13) is unthinkable for a Christian.

Paul tells us that we have been saved by grace through faith (Ephesians 2:8–10). As he says in verse 9: "Not by works, so that no one can boast." No part of our salvation is because of what we do, because if it were, Paul says, human beings would boast. Anyone who believes that any part of their salvation is due to the things they do or don't do will inevitably wind up boasting.

If we think we have anything at all to do with our salvation, we will strut and swagger. We will get puffed up if we believe our truth, our doctrines, our dogmas, our ceremonies, and our rituals are better than someone else's. If we are convinced that we have anything to do with our salvation, we will brag that our music and hymns and our times or seasons in which we worship God are the best, if not the only way to worship God.

If we are deceived into thinking that what we do earns us salvation, we may begin to believe that God has given us superior knowledge and esoteric insights. If we think that we have any part in our salvation, we will parade around, claiming that our church is bigger, our pastor is more "anointed" and our congregation is more spirit-filled than others.

If our brand of religion is threatened by the implications of freedom in Christ, we will attack. *Bad News Religion* protects itself at all costs. The first priority is to protect the institution and organization, not to feed and nurture the sheep of God's pasture. Since grace is an obstacle, legalism will vilify and condemn.

Bad News Religion drugs us, mesmerizing us, blinding us to

God's grace and intoxicating us on the heady wine of the works of our own hands. Works and deeds lead to arrogance, my-church-is-better-than-your-church exclusivism and smug self righteousness.

If we think that anything we do has any part in earning our salvation, we wind up bragging that our righteousness is based upon our goodness. The lyrics of an old song provide a parody of this self-righteous externalism—"We don't smoke, we don't chew, and we don't go with the girls that do." We wind up knee deep in some religious swamp, enveloped by legalism, congratulating ourselves about what good boys and girls we are and assuming that God must be so pleased with us (and of course he is so shocked and appalled with everyone else!).

THE CHURCH LADY

Now this may come as a huge shock to you, and you may not ever read another word I write, but confession is good for the soul. I was a huge fan of the old television program, "Saturday Night Live." I laughed myself silly at the exploits of John Belushi as the Samurai man. I loved Roseanne Rosanna-danna, Father Guido Sarducci and many other recurring skits—but I howled at the biting humor of the Church Lady.

Dana Carvey played the Church Lady, breaking into what he called "the superior dance" when he portrayed the Church Lady as having done some righteous deed. When the Church Lady did something that she felt elevated her above all of the other religious ladies she knew, she broke into the superior dance, smug self-righteousness oozing out of every dance step.

I realize that what I've just said puts me on many radar screens. I've confessed not only to watching "Saturday Night Live" but enjoying a stereotype of "good Christians." Grace is one thing, but the Church Lady?

Fact is, I enjoyed the Church Lady (and still do when I see a re-run or watch a video) because she reminds me of the legalistic antics that used to convince me of my supposed superiority. The Church Lady makes me laugh at my own religious posturings.

One of the Church Lady's favorite moralizing "summary judg-ments" was: "Isn't that special?" Of course, Christians are special, but we are special only because Jesus is matchless and unequaled. God credits the uniqueness of Jesus to us because of his grace.

But here's the paradox. Those who have accepted God's grace do not promote themselves or their incorporated group. Those who are truly unique in Christ do not trumpet their own merit or strut their stuff in a spiritual superior dance. Authentic Christians allow their lives to be reflections of Christ so that others might come to know the Lord.

As Christians we are not defined by what we do or don't do. We are defined by what Christ accomplishes in and through us. In Ephesians Paul says:

> We are God's workmanship, created in Christ Jesus to do good works, which God prepared in advance for us to do.
> —EPHESIANS 2:10

We're not saved *by* works, rather we are saved *for* works. The issue is all about who gets the credit. We don't get the credit for our salva-tion, and we never will. All of the credit and all of the glory goes to God. Nothing we can ever do will ever be worth enough to earn any-thing from God. If we have accepted Jesus Christ and understand the enormity of what he has done for us, we will not brag about the inconsequential things we do or don't do because we realize how insignificant and petty they are compared to the righteousness of

Jesus Christ. If we truly understand and live by and in God's amazing grace, we will not break into superior dances.

We cannot claim one ounce of credit for our salvation. God insists on our unconditional surrender to any claim we might have to any part of our salvation. That's part of what repentance and accepting Jesus Christ is all about. That's also why so many people are reluctant to "surrender all"—as we sing in that grand old hymn. While Christians are not defined by what they do or don't do, they are defined by what Jesus does within them. Humanly, we don't like the idea of being given something by grace, free of charge, which we didn't earn. Being told that our salvation is given to us because of God's goodness doesn't appeal to us. We like to think that we will earn our salvation because of our goodness. If God gives us something that we did not participate in, or contribute to, we feel obligated—and we don't like to feel obligated to anyone. Easy-believism is a lie, but don't let anyone tell you easy-believism is one and the same as God's grace.

God can never be obligated to us because of some good thing we do or perform. But we are obligated to God. Jesus Christ has redeemed us from the slavery of sin; he's purchased us with his blood. Because of, and through Christ, God will work in us "to will and act according to his good purpose" (Philippians 2:13).

GOD LETS PEOPLE "GET AWAY" WITH SIN

What would you think if I told you that I believed that two of the most notorious butchers and mass murderers of our times, Adolf Hitler and Joseph Stalin, are now in heaven? Suppose I had some kind of evidence that had surfaced that proves beyond a shadow of a doubt that before they died, both of these men repented of their sins? What if we had proof that they had actually accepted Jesus Christ shortly before they died? Do you think someone who had been that evil in his life could repent on his deathbed? What about all that bad stuff he did? Will he be able to get away with it?

Christianity presents us with a dilemma, as understood by our grace-less human heart (Jeremiah 17:9). God lets people get away with sin. That is, at least from our perspective it seems that God lets people get away with sin. It doesn't appear that God always makes them pay. Now, for the record, this is just hypothetical. I don't think that Stalin or Hitler repented before they died; yet it presents us with a good theological question.

What if God did forgive Hitler and Stalin? How would you feel about that? The Bible does tell us in Luke 23:39-43 about another notorious person who died on a cross alongside Jesus Christ. The thief on the cross was saved just as he died, in spite of being a criminal. Jesus, who had the authority to do so, saved the thief on the cross.

How *do* you feel about that? You probably don't like to think about it. After all, the thief probably did lead a wild and unrestrained life, doing whatever he wanted. After walking on the wild side all his life, the thief repented at the very end—a deathbed repentance. And he's saved, according to the Bible, just the same as someone who never missed going to church for 30 years. Is that fair?

You may remember the story of the prodigal son, and the older brother who stayed home and didn't join his younger brother wasting his inheritance on a wild bash and spending spree. The older brother who remained behind, working hard in his father's fields, didn't like it when his younger brother returned to a forgiving father. Grace was freely given with no sacrifices to offer, no candles to light, no penance to pay, and no deeds to perform. No stipulations. Just flat out forgiven. The older brother was not amused.

From our human perspective there is something scandalous

about God's grace. But the fact is, this is what the gospel of Jesus Christ teaches—whether we like it or not. No matter what anyone does, he or she can receive God's grace. No matter how many bad and evil things you have done or how diabolical your sins, God's grace can cover you. No matter how much pain and suffering you have caused, God's grace will forgive you. All you need to do is accept and believe the fact that only Jesus Christ can save you.

We like to think that God will save us because we've been good religious people. God saves us because he is good. And that's the end of *Bad News Religion* and the beginning of the gospel.

How Religion Can Overwhelm Authentic Christianity

Paul instructs us to:

> See to it that no one takes you captive through hollow and deceptive philosophy, which depends on human tradition and the basic principles of this world rather than on Christ.
>
> —Colossians 2:8

Religion and legalism impose a host of humanly derived regulations that, according to religion, will set us apart, make us special and unique, and give us favor with God that will be denied to others. Religion causes us to look to duties and deeds as the basis of our relationship with God rather than his providential grace, which alone saves us. In the second chapter of Colossians Paul tells us:

> Since you died with Christ to the basic principles of this world, why, as though you still belonged to it, do you submit to its rules: "Do not *handle!* Do not *taste!* Do not

touch!"? These are all destined to perish with use, because they are based on human commands and teachings. Such regulations indeed have an appearance of wisdom, with their self-imposed worship, their false humility and their harsh treatment of the body, but they lack any value in restraining sensual indulgence.

—COLOSSIANS 2:20–23 *(emphasis added)*

Paul offers us a list of telltale signs that religion has overwhelmed our worship:

- Do not handle

- Do not taste

- Do not touch

- Human commands and teachings

- Regulations

- Appearance of wisdom

- Self-imposed worship

- False humility

- Harsh treatment of the body

Bad News Religion offers us a package of behaviors that convince us that we are being righteous and holy, that not only will God be impressed, but so will other human beings! Performance-based religion offers us the "benefit" that religious stuff we do and perform will "have an appearance of wisdom." Impressing other human beings can be a seductive motivation that can lead us to a lifetime of religious obligation, thinking all the while that we are doing exactly what God wants.

One of the hardest things for any of us to do is to distinguish between what other human beings tell us is righteous, proper, and appropriate, and what God tells us. We often confuse what the Bible says and what people tell us it says. Religious legalism disorients us, and our chief concern then becomes what people see us doing and not doing, as opposed to being content with the unconditional love, acceptance, and forgiveness God offers us freely.

Legalism may temporarily put a lid on some immoral and sinful behavior—but rules and restrictions are not the answer for sin! Can you see the fatal attraction? The whole focus is all about us, and what we do and don't do. When *Bad News Religion* seduces a child of God who is free in Christ, relationship can quickly move from a focus on the God of the Bible to a relationship with a god or gods of humanly derived religion.

In an attempt to turn us away from authentic Christianity *Bad News Religion* makes our worship into idolatry. It seduces us into making a golden calf from the things we do, and then encourages us to bow down and worship the works of our own hands. In the early years of the 21st century North Americans are just as busy making our golden calves as the nation of Israel was while they waited for Moses to come down from the mountain.

For example, can you imagine the shock it would be for some Christians if they discovered that God was not an American, and not only that, not even a Republican? What will happen if some good religious folks arrive in heaven and discover that God plays cards and enjoys a good joke? Will they stay or will they depart for a more righteous place?

Several years ago I was helping in a ministry of racial reconciliation with an African-American pastor friend of mine. When churches across North America that were concerned about this issue invited us, my friend and I would speak, as black and white ministers who believe in the same gospel of Jesus Christ. The mere fact of having two ministers share a pulpit, one ivory and the other ebony (as we joked), helped people realize that black Christians and white Christians could actually worship together.

I often told these church congregations that I had a recurring dream, and in my dream my friend and I both died within a few days of each other. When we arrived in heaven our first request was to see God. St. Peter told us that God was busy, but if we would have a seat in the waiting room he would be with us in a while. So, we sat down and started looking through all the back copies of *The Plain Truth* magazine that St. Peter keeps in his reception area (a joke within a joke!).

So there we were—two middle aged men, one black and one white, waiting to meet God in heaven. After about an hour or so we heard sounds coming from down the street. The footsteps we heard had to be God—they were authoritative, powerful, and they got louder and louder as he approached us. The footsteps continued to get progressively louder and closer until they stopped on the other side of the reception area.

We both looked at each other as the doorknob started to turn. Of course both of us were absolutely certain that God was an American, and that he would like baseball, apple pie, hamburgers, and would stand up for the *Star Spangled Banner* with his hand covering his heart. However, my friend was convinced that God was black, and I was convinced that God was white. We were amazed when the door opened, God walked in and said, "Buenos dias, mis amigos!"

God has an amazing way of helping us enlarge our perspectives. There was a time when I viewed Catholics and Pentecostals as fringe Christians (this perception and attitude coming from someone who believed in and taught Armstrongism for decades!). I am pleased to say that I now have some dear Pentecostal and Catholic friends. God has helped me off my religious high horse. He has changed my narrow, restrictive, and exclusive ideas. I now realize that the unkempt homeless person who tries to wash my windshield as I wait at a traffic light on my way to church might actually have a closer relationship with God than I do. Have you ever considered that God might enjoy an occasional beer or glass of wine, that he might leap onto the dance floor of heaven from time to time or that he really does enjoy some contemporary music?

There's an old story about God and judgment day. According to the story God has everyone who has ever lived gather before him and tells them that he's not really going to judge them by grace— instead the basis of their judgment will be how well they followed the non-essential unbiblical traditions they believed in and religiously followed.

The angels begin to read the roll call of religions and Christian denominations along with their distinctives. All who failed to live up to the extra-biblical rules and regulations of the religion, sect, group, or fellowship they were members of are dismissed. As the roll call of world religions, Christian churches, and denominations of every size and shape continues only a small number from each group remains—just a handful from every group were able to be faithful to all humanly imposed rules they tried to follow. Finally, when all have been judged by standards that God never authorized or directed, the story relates that God surveys this small group of people.

He considers the grim-faced, smug, hard-nosed, self-righteous group that have somehow managed to carefully obey all religious and denominational regulations, and begins to contemplate spending eternity in a joyless heaven where laughter is nonexistent and where everyone will take themselves far too seriously.

He looks over to the angels and says, "Bring everybody back. It's got to be by grace. No way will I be able to spend eternity with these folks."

THE TIMELESS MESSAGE OF AMOS

Like 21st century North Americans, the Hebrew prophet Amos lived in a time of prosperity. Amos and most of his Israelite countrymen enjoyed good times and many prided themselves on their religious deeds. The upper class had achieved much of their prosperity at the expense of the poor. The rich got richer, and the poor got poorer.

At the time of Amos, the Israelites clung to the rituals of their faith. They were comfortable doing what they had always done; secure in thinking that God was happy with them because they did stuff he wanted them to do. As long as they fulfilled the basic requirements of their religion, the people of Israel felt that they pleased and appeased God.

God sent Amos with a message the people found hard to accept. God told them they were deceived, that while they thought they were doing all the right things to please him, their hearts were far from him. That message is just as true and applicable today! With that in mind, consider part of Amos' message:

> I hate, I despise your religious feasts; I cannot stand your assemblies. Even though you bring me burnt offerings and grain offerings, I will not accept them. Though you bring choice fellowship offerings, I will have no regard for them. Away with the noise of your songs! I will not listen to the music of your harps. But let justice roll on like a river, right-eousness like a never-failing stream! Did you bring me sac-rifices and offerings forty years in the desert, O house of Israel? You have lifted up the *shrine* of your king, the

pedestal of your idols, the *star* of your god—which you
made for yourselves.

—AMOS 5:21–26 (EMPHASIS ADDED)

Notice the words that God inspired Amos to use when describing how people deify religious rites and rituals. We make shrines of humanly produced righteousness. We place the idols of our traditions on pedestals, and the stars we admire and worship are the gods we create.

When Jesus Christ alone is our guide, we are not concerned with human righteousness and our own religious reputation. Legalism will never produce God's righteousness and justice—they come from him, free of charge, without deeds we must perform to earn it—God's righteousness and justice come by his grace alone. But when righteousness is measured by human tradition, it provides an excuse for self-centeredness and arrogance (see Matthew 15:6).

When religious legalism is our foundational guide for belief and practice, we can become heartless and uncaring, cold and calculating people whose god is our own strict standards of behavior rather than the suffering Servant, the Lamb of God, the Good Samaritan, who loves unconditionally. The people of Israel to whom Amos ministered were smug and self-satisfied because they felt they were doing all of the right things and few of the wrong things, but at the same time they were grievously oppressing the poor. Legalism deceives us into thinking that if we do all of the right religious rituals and obey all of the religious rules God will wink at our shortcomings.

Religion that uses the name of Christ should be encouraging us to be more like Jesus. But much of the time it does the precise opposite. Some Christians leave the distinct impression that Christians are angry, mean spirited, close-minded, aggressive, critical people who condemn those who are not exactly like themselves.

God is calling us to have a personal relationship with him, a heart-relationship. God offers us everything we will ever need through his grace. All we need to do is repent, surrender, and give up thinking that we can ever get any credit for what God alone can do. This means we need to repent of *Bad News Religion*. We need to turn away from those who beckon to us to condemn others. Jesus did not boycott anyone; he reached out and touched those no one else would. Jesus loved the unloved, the lost, the forsaken, and the abandoned. He is the Good Samaritan who stops and helps (Luke 10:33–34), compared with the priests of religion who pass by on the other side.

If we accept God's grace, we will reject legalism and attempts to turn us into enforcers of religious rites, rules, and regulations. There is, after all, only one God. Only one Savior. The one true God is not the property of *Bad News Religion*. He is not dispensed in the traditions and teachings of human religion, nor is he solely represented by any one movement, group, or church. Our Lord and Savior saves us, and he does so in spite of the best efforts of legalism to enslave us.

WINNING THE LOTTERY

Let me give you an illustration of God's grace. Imagine a New York City diner. It's breakfast time, and the diner is crowded with people inhaling their breakfast, in a hurry to go to work. A New York City policeman is having coffee along with his partner. As he finishes, he reaches into his pocket to pay the bill and to leave a tip, but he finds that he only has enough money to pay for the coffee. There's not enough in his pocket to tip Yvonne, the waitress.

Charlie, the cop, is embarrassed, so he offers Yvonne a choice. He promises to return the next day with double the usual tip, or he offers another option. He promises to split his lottery ticket with her (and that's the reason he doesn't have any money for the tip—because he just purchased the ticket earlier that morning). So in full view of his partner and other diners, he takes the lottery ticket out of his wallet, and he holds it up.

If Yvonne chooses this option for her tip, Charlie promises to equally divide any money he wins from the drawing (if his numbers are drawn that evening), with Yvonne.

Yvonne, the waitress, is having a bad day. She hates her job. Her husband left her a few weeks ago, but not before running up the balance on all their credit cards. Yesterday, Yvonne was in court declaring bankruptcy.

It looks like she'll be in debt the rest of her life. Things couldn't get any worse, and now Charlie, the cop, doesn't even have enough money for a tip. Instead of a tip, the cheap skate is offering to split his could-be, would-be, hoped-for lottery winnings with her.

Yvonne sighs and good-naturedly says, "All right—fine." She accepts the offer. You might be way ahead of me on this story. Especially if you saw the movie *It Could Happen to You.* The improbable and the impossible happen, according to the movie.

That night Charlie's lottery ticket wins the grand prize of four million dollars. The next morning Charlie comes to the diner to give Yvonne the good news. Charlie already had a fight with his wife who is outraged that he agreed to give a waitress half his lottery winnings. But Charlie's an honest guy, and, after all, there were witnesses to Charlie's offer.

You can imagine Yvonne's reaction to this news. At first, utter disbelief spreads across her face. "No! No! Why are you doing this to me? Why are you playing this cruel joke on me telling me that I won half the lottery last night? This could not happen to me. Nothing good ever happens to me. This is just too good to be true!"

Then slowly, as Charlie insists that he's not joking, a tiny flicker of hope registers deep inside of Yvonne. She dares to believe that it just might be true. But disbelief continues to flood through her. After all it was only yesterday she had accepted her fate that she would probably be bankrupt the rest of her life. But Charlie's smile and genuine excitement, along with his insistence that what he's saying is true, gradually melts Yvonne's skepticism. Charlie says, "It can happen. It has happened. It has happened to you."

As Yvonne screams with delight, dancing around the diner to the cheers and applause of her regular customers, she asks Charlie, "Why? You didn't even have to tell me you won the lottery. You could have kept it all for yourself. Why are you doing this?"

Charlie, the honest cop, simply answers, "Because a promise is a promise."

We all know God's promise to us. We memorized it a long time ago. But do we believe it? The promise is in John 3:16.

> For God so loved the world, that he gave his one and only son that whoever believes in him shall not perish, but have eternal life.

God's grace seems to be too good to be true. It's hard to accept and believe. In fact, some people will not accept God's grace for that reason. They cannot accept what they see as something for nothing and therefore feel obligated. They have to do their part. They would rather go on trying to earn God's grace than believe that God has actually given it to them without strings, without obligation.

The rest of the movie, *It Could Happen to You,* also has implications for Christians. Yvonne's life is changed forever, and she cannot help but be attracted to Charlie, who is an honest, generous, and loving person. But Charlie is married and faithful to his wife. Hollywood makes the story turn out well. Charlie's greedy, bitter wife divorces him, largely because he gave away one-half of his lottery winnings. In the end Charlie and Yvonne wind up together.

And interestingly, according to the movie at least, Yvonne doesn't just take the money and run anymore than authentic Christians take God's grace and run when we comprehend the riches of his grace. Yvonne doesn't want simply what Charlie gave her; she wants to be with him for the rest of her life. This giving, honest, promise-keeping person was truly unlike anyone she had ever known.

Yvonne doesn't start to practice "easy-believism." The grace that has been given to her does not encourage her to be a permissive person, taking advantage of the love and generosity given to her.

Of course, this movie is an imperfect and flawed picture of our relationship with our Lord and Savior. Winning the lottery cannot be compared to being given salvation by grace. But since we humans are convinced that money can rescue us, solve our problems, and change our lives, the picture of someone who wins the lottery and without obligation gives one-half of the jackpot to someone else helps us visualize the riches of God's grace.

As grace-filled Christians, we don't serve God out of fear, worried about what he might do to us if we disobey. We don't obey him so that we can earn his love, so that he might then save us or feel obligated to save us because we've done so many good things. We obey God because he has overwhelmed us with his love.

We're all like Yvonne, the waitress in the diner. We have more bad days than good ones. In fact, we're having a tough life. We are deeply in debt, without a snowball's chance in hell of paying all of our spiritual bills. God comes to us in our sin, in our need, in our moral bankruptcy, in the desperately hopeless condition in which we find ourselves, and for no apparent reason he loves us.

He loves us in spite of who we are. God has nothing to gain from loving us. We cannot offer him anything that is equal to his love in return. God loves us because he is who he is, not because we are who we are.

That's what grace is all about. That's God's amazing grace. And so the question: "Since God saves us by grace, since God loves me unconditionally, why should I even try? Why should I obey him? Why should I be good?"

The answer is obvious, isn't it? When someone has been that lavish in his riches toward us, we love him. We will do anything for him. The thought of not being with him, obeying him, and being devoted to him for the rest of our lives is unthinkable. We obey him because of his grace and because of what he has done for us.

So does God's grace lead us to permissiveness? Paul explains:

> For the grace of God that brings salvation has appeared to all men. It teaches us to say "No" to ungodliness and worldly passions, and to live self-controlled, upright and godly lives in this present age, while we wait for the blessed hope—the glorious appearing of our great God and Savior, Jesus Christ, who gave himself for us to redeem us from all wickedness and to purify for himself a people that are his very own, eager to do what is good.
>
> TITUS 2:11–14

Chapter Eight—Review and Recap

Doing whatever we want. The opposite extreme of religious legalism is easy-believism or permissiveness. Permissiveness is not good news—it, like *Bad News Religion,* is the enemy of God's grace.

Boasting because of our deeds. If we think we have anything at all to do with our salvation, we will get puffed up about our truth, our doctrines, our dogmas, our ceremonies, and our rituals.

Doing whatever Jesus wants. Christians are not defined by what they do or don't do. They are defined by what Jesus does within them and through them.

Saved *for* works. Christians obey God because they have been saved, not in order to be saved. We are not saved *by* works, we are saved *for* works.

"Getting away" with sin. God's grace presents us with a dilemma—it seems to us that God lets people get away with sin. It's been called the scandal of God's grace.

Duties and deeds. God does not save us because we've been good. God saves us because he is good. *Bad News Religion* causes us to look to duties and deeds as a basis of our relationship with God-rather than his grace, which alone saves us.

9

Joe the Pastor and Joe the Cab Driver

"When the average non-Christian hears the word 'Christian,' he or she doesn't think of the body of Christ or the church at large or of followers of Christ in all cultures, classes, races, and nationalities. The person is more likely to have in mind a kind of American cultural Christianity that is a composite of what has surfaced in the media in this country in the last 15 to 20 years—a stilted stereotype at best. Whether we like it or not, we have been branded with an image, and the image is not a good one."

—*Fearless Faith,* John Fischer

"There is perhaps no better proof for the existence of God than the fact that year after year he survives the way his professional friends promote him. If there are people who remain unconvinced, let them tune in their TVs to almost any of the big-time pulpit-pounders almost any Sunday morning of the year."

—*Whistling in the Dark,* Frederick Buechner

JESUS TOLD STORIES to help us understand the good news he proclaimed. Story after story gives us word pictures of the reality of God's kingdom, the power of his grace and the depth of his love. In one of these stories Jesus taught us one of the important differences between religion and Christianity. People who are trapped by religion often become *"confident of their own righteousness"* (Luke 18:9) and look down on others.

We know the story as the Parable of the Pharisee and the Publican, found in Luke 18:9–14. The two leading roles written into this story by the divine author couldn't be more different. First let's consider the Pharisee. Pharisees were extremely diligent about observing the law, perhaps more than any one religious group that has ever lived.

There was a downside to all their attention to the law. Pharisees could become terribly impressed with themselves. They knew that they were obedient to the law, and their careful devotion often made them smug, arrogant, and hard to live with.

Pharisees were hard on themselves, and just as tough on others. They tended to have little time, mercy, or compassion for those they viewed as slackers—people who didn't measure up to their standards.

We often sum this up by calling the Pharisees self-righteous. And of course we delight in reviewing their religious idiosyncrasies because they are not at all like our own religious peculiarities, are they? It's ironic that some of our critiques of the Pharisees are often delivered from pulpits in our own legalistic swamps, from the bondage of our spiritual prison cells, as we desperately try to assure ourselves that we are not modern day Pharisees.

The Pharisees are not extinct. Performance religion flourishes. Modern Pharisees are alive and well, infiltrating and infecting Christendom, threatening to lead us away from the Incarnation of grace to the incarceration of legalism.

The publican that Jesus mentioned in the parable was at the other end of the religious spectrum—the Pharisees were admired and publicans were despised. Publican is an old English word for tax collector. Of course, tax collectors are never well liked or respected in any society, but in the Holy Land at the time of Christ they were the lowest of the low. Tax collectors were Jews who collected taxes from fellow Jews on behalf of the Romans, the occupying military power.

Most Jews at the time of Christ did not believe that humans could sink any lower than being a tax collector for the Romans. They were thought to be thieves, because it was common knowledge that the Romans allowed tax collectors to "skim" some of the money they collected. They were viewed as traitors, because they were collecting money for a foreign power that was oppressing the Jews.

So Jesus set up this story with a recognized, "holy-Joe" righteous person, who was immediately identified as the good guy in the story by his listeners, and a person whose profession immediately earmarked him for scorn and ridicule, the bad guy in the eyes of Jesus' audience—the hero and the villain.

But as often happens with the gospel, our immediate human impression and judgment is very often the diametric opposite of God's perspective. In choosing these two people to play these roles Jesus was turning the tables on his listeners, setting them (and us!) up to immediately identify with the wrong person in order to emphasize the moral of the story.

Of course, because we know the moral of the story we immediately identify with the Publican, but for someone who had never heard the story, it would have been far different. The story is simple:

- Both men, the one assumed to be righteous and the one assumed to be unrighteous, went up to the temple to pray (verse 10).

- The Pharisee prayed "about himself" (verse 11).

- The Pharisee was thankful that he was not like other men who were sinners (verse 11).

- The Pharisee reminded God of his good deeds (verse 12).

- The tax collector "stood at a distance" (verse 13).

- The tax collector could not even look up at heaven in prayer and simply asked God to forgive him, an acknowledged sinner (verse 13).

- The Pharisee seemed to feel no need for forgiveness, while the tax collector knew exactly who he was—a sinner—and what his need was—God's mercy.

- Jesus concluded the story, giving us the moral—"For everyone who exalts himself will be humbled, and he who humbles himself will be exalted" (verse 14).

THE PASTOR AND THE CAB DRIVER

A pastor dies and finds himself waiting in line at the Pearly Gates of heaven. He is standing right behind a guy who is wearing sunglasses and a loud Hawaiian print shirt and smoking a cigar. After about an hour or so the pastor and the cigar smoker move to the front of the line, and St. Peter motions to the sunglasses-wearing individual, who is definitely not dressed for success, to come forward.

Peter says, "Name and earthly occupation please." The guy wearing the loud shirt says, "Joe Furrillo, taxi driver, the Bronx, New York."

Peter smiles, double checks the computer monitor in front of him and says, "Joe, welcome. We've been expecting you. Take this golden staff and these silk robes, go into the changing room over there, and enter the kingdom of heaven."

Peter turns and looks at the pastor, who is the next person in line, and says, "Next!"

The pastor confidently walks forward and Peter says, "Name and earthly occupation please." The pastor stands up straight, and booms out, "I am the Right Reverend Presiding Bishop Dr. Joe Schmoe, pastor of St. Muckedy Muck's on Park Avenue for 47 years."

St. Peter frowns, looks a little bored and starts searching his computer. After a few minutes he looks up with a tired and resigned look and says, "O.K. You're in. Take this cotton robe and wooden staff and enter the kingdom of heaven. You can change in the changing room over there."

The pastor says, "Wait a minute! The guy ahead of me was a taxi driver—he gets a silk robe and a golden staff—and I was a pastor of one of the most important mega-churches in one of the largest cities on earth for almost 50 years and all I get is this cheap robe and a wooden staff? There must be some mistake. Check that computer again."

Peter says, "Oh, no. There's no mistake. Entrance into the kingdom is by God's grace. So you're in—in spite of yourself. But you are very impressed with your performance, so because you seem to prefer it that way, your robe and staff were selected based on your works."

Then Peter says, with a slight smile, "Not only that, we took something else into consideration. When you preached, people went to sleep. When Joe the taxi driver drove, people prayed!"

Five Questions—Legalism or God's Grace?

Even though many Christians completely accept God's grace, and that the gospel of Jesus Christ is all about grace, many are still tormented by thoughts that God is not pleased with them. Many who know that they cannot possibly earn their salvation still think that God has some kind of big scoreboard in heaven. Some perceive God's kingdom of heaven as a place where angels scurry around updating our daily spiritual progress so that God will always be able to know just how well we are doing (as if he wouldn't know about us without the scoreboard).

Some visualize the throne room of heaven as a place somewhat like the New York Stock Exchange. They see continuous electronic reports scrolling across screens on the walls, with *endless updates of our spiritual performance constantly being reviewed by God and millions of angels.*

There are times when even those of us who know that salvation is by grace alone, faith alone, and Christ alone are plagued by mental images of God as some kind of coach, with a clip board and stop watch, monitoring our daily achievements and short-comings.

Even though many Christians completely accept God's grace, and that the gospel of Jesus Christ is all about grace, many are still tormented by thoughts that God is not pleased with them.

Even when God has revealed his wonderful and priceless grace to us, lavishing his goodness and love upon us, we still deal with perceptions and stereotypes of who God really is. We want to believe that salvation and our relationship with God is all about Jesus and not about us, but performance-based religion is embedded in our minds.

In the name of Jesus Christ legalistic religion hammers us with the idea that we need to do more and more—and unless we do, God will not be happy. We are easy prey for this manipulation because the virus of *Bad News Religion* lurks in our souls, waiting for times when we are down and depressed. The goal of legalism is to restrict, control, and enslave you and me. God's grace, by contrast, sets us free.

Paul begins chapter three of the book of Galatians by asking five questions of the Galatians, who had been bewitched, hoodwinked, and seduced by religious legalism, after Paul had preached God's gracious gospel to them. Here they are:

1) In the first verse of chapter three, Paul says,

> You foolish Galatians, who has bewitched you?

The Galatians had fallen for the oldest line in the book of *Bad News Religion*. "Sure God loves you, but you have to prove it to him. He loves you when you are good, when you do the right things. So you need to show him why he should keep loving you..."

The truth is, of course, that God loves us because he is good, and in Christ he has demonstrated how much he loves us, giving us salvation because of Jesus' work on the cross for us.

2) Then, in the second verse, Paul asks,

> I would like to learn just one thing from you: Did you receive the Spirit by observing the law, or by believing what you heard?

Paul is attacking the core teaching of the seductive legalism that had bewitched the Galatians. He is reminding them that God had already saved them, already given them the Holy Spirit, by his grace, without cost or obligation. He is reminding the Galatians that God adopted them as his very own children because they had faith and trust in Jesus Christ, not because of their performance.

3) In the third verse Paul asks,

> Are you so foolish? After beginning with the Spirit, are you now trying to attain your goal by human effort?

Paul cuts to the core issue with incisive logic. Did the Galatians think that God had loved them and showered them with his grace in spite of who they were, but now he would only keep loving them if they earned his love? The legalist who is trapped by religion will almost never say, "I am saved only by what I do and accomplish on my own." Slaves of *Bad News Religion* will usually say, "Oh sure, salvation is by God's grace alone, but he expects me to produce and perform in order to maintain my salvation, so that I can remain in his grace. God saves me initially, but it's up to me to remain that way."

4) In verse four Paul reminds the Galatians,

> Have you suffered so much for nothing—if it really was for nothing?

Paul tells the Galatians they had made a commitment to renounce the works of the flesh. They had once rejected the religious fallacy that we humans can control and manipulate our spiritual destiny. They had accepted authentic Christianity that teaches that Jesus alone saves us, and that nothing we do has any bearing whatsoever on our salvation.

Rejecting the idea that our human efforts have any bearing on our relationship with God is hard—it involves sacrifice and suffering. We must surrender and repent, accepting Jesus who can do for us what we can never do for ourselves.

5) And finally, in verse five Paul repeats what he had asked in the second verse:

> Does God give you his Spirit and work miracles among you because you observe the law, or because you believe what you heard?

Paul demands that salvation is considered either on the basis of what we do, because of our devotion and obedience—OR—that salvation is a gift, by God's grace, because we believe and trust in Jesus Christ. Paul does not allow for some middle ground of both/and. That non-existent middle ground was the basis of the Galatian heresy, the unbiblical notion that salvation is by our obedience to the law plus God's grace. Paul says, NO—you must choose between your goodness and righteousness and God's.

Is It Really True That God Will Not Love You Unless You. . . .?

The subtle deception that human works and deeds have anything to do with our salvation has always been the biggest obstacle to the gospel of Jesus Christ. Salvation is by grace alone, by faith alone, and by Jesus Christ alone. *Bad News Religion* contorts and twists the gospel, by placing the focus on issues as a basis for salvation such as:

- A specific way and time in which we must be baptized.

- Specific dates and times when we have to go to church, and specific dates and times we should not go to church.

- A specific percentage of income that God requires us to pay to a particular church or denomination.

- You should only read and study King James translations. Other translations are pagan and even perverted.

- Women may not wear jeans or pants, or dresses that are higher than ankle-length.

- Only "approved" hymns may be sung in church.

- You may not wear jewelry of any kind—it is vanity. Some even teach that this religious prohibition applies to wedding rings.

- You cannot eat certain foods, which have been decided upon by your pastor or the founder of your movement, group or denomination.

- You should never go to movies—or at least not those which are not on the acceptable list your pastor or denomination provides.

- You may not marry anyone who is not in your specific church or denomination.

- You may never drink any alcohol of any kind.

- You must attend all activities and services of your church— you must be there whenever the "door is open."

Paul counters all of this "stuff" by saying,

> It is for freedom that Christ has set us free. Stand firm, then, and do not let yourselves be burdened again by a yoke of slavery.
>
> —GALATIANS 5:1

Paul pleaded that we accept the freedom that Christ offers and that we never allow religious bondage to overcome us. Paul insisted that ". . . there is now no condemnation for those who are in Christ Jesus..." (Romans 8:1).

THE GRACE OF LES MISERABLES

You may have either read Victor's Hugo's *Les Miserables* or seen the musical stage presentation. It is a powerful and enduring story of grace. Jean Valjean receives an unjust sentence for stealing a loaf of bread to feed his sister's starving children. He spends 19 years in prison, and in the process becomes an embittered man.

When Valjean is released, he finds out that life is hard for an ex-con. No one trusts him, and when he does find some work, he is cheated out of fair wages by those who take advantage of his status as a felon. His bitterness grows and deepens.

One night, desperate for a place to stay, Valjean asks to stay with a Catholic bishop. The difficult circumstances in which he found himself, the bitterness he was dealing with, combined with the temptation of the wealth that Valjean saw in the bishop's home proved to be too much for him. Valjean gave in to his human nature, and as he left the bishop's home he stole some of the bishop's silver.

Valjean's sin was quickly discovered. The police apprehended him, discovered the silver and took him back to the bishop's house for a positive identification of the criminal they now had under arrest.

When the bishop saw Valjean, much to everyone's surprise, the bishop picked up two silver candlesticks and brought them to Valjean. "You forgot these," he said, implying that all of the silver Valjean had in his possession was a gift from the bishop.

Here is the centerpiece of Hugo's masterpiece. After the police leave, the bishop says, "Jean Valjean, my brother, you no longer belong to evil, but to good. It is your soul I buy back from you."

This unbelievable, amazing miracle—this completely unexpected miracle of God's grace changes the life of Jean Valjean. He becomes a Christian. He assumes a new identity, works hard to become the owner of a factory and one day the mayor of a town. He knows that he is the recipient of God's amazing grace and passes that grace on in his life. He serves others, building schools and helping the sick and the poor.

But that's not the end of the story. While Valjean is in prison a guard named Javert makes life miserable for him. He now vows to do all he can to ensure that Valjean returns to prison. Javert knows no mercy, no leniency and certainly does not understand grace. Javert knows only one kind of justice—a strict, careful, and literal application of the law. An eye for an eye.

But Javert is himself a prisoner—a prisoner of the law. His devotion to legalism and to all of the nuances and specifics of the law blinds him to the reality of a loving and merciful God. He believes Valjean is getting away with something and devotes his life to putting him behind bars once again.

Toward the end of the story Javert finds himself a captive, and those who have Javert bound with ropes offer Valjean a gun and invite him to kill his adversary. Valjean cuts the ropes that bind his tormentor and sets him free.

Another miracle. Another act of grace. But this time the result is different. Javert cannot comprehend mercy, and he certainly cannot accept it. His legalistic world continues to enslave him, so much so that he takes his own life.

Valjean accepts the grace that was offered to him and becomes a child of God, living a new life. Javert rejects the grace that Valjean passes on, and the torment of his bondage to legalism leads him to commit suicide.

It is not easy to accept God's grace. Accepting Jesus Christ is itself a repudiation of our world and its religion. Accepting God's grace is humbling, and leads to deep repentance as we realize, on the one hand, our inadequacy and on the other, God's perfect love. God's grace turns human ideas about fairness and justice upside down. God's grace changes everything. There are many people like Javert who cannot accept God's grace and will not allow themselves to be freed from the bondage of their lives. They choose slavery to sin and our world instead of the freedom in Christ God offers us by his grace.

The good news of the gospel of Jesus Christ is that God has found us and that he has delivered us from sin, not because we are good, but because he is good. We are saved by grace alone, through faith alone, and in Christ alone. That's incredible, amazing good news!

Chapter Nine—Review and Recap

Bad news in the Bible. The Pharisees and the Galatian heresy are two biblical examples of *Bad News Religion*. Both groups emphasized observance over belief—performance to the exclusion of God's grace.

Towing the line. Like Phariseeism, *Bad News Religion* breeds long lists of rules and regulations that people are convinced they must obey for God to be pleased with them.

Grace is not easy. The act of accepting God's grace means rejecting the standards and perspectives of our world and its religion.

God doesn't keep score. Even when we accept God's grace we can have mental images of a heaven where big scoreboards and continuous electronic reports provide endless updates of our spiritual performance so that God and millions of angels can constantly review our progress.

10

THE DAY GRACE WAS PREACHED AT FIRST DUCK CHURCH

"Somehow throughout history the church has managed to gain a reputation for its ungrace. As a little English girl prayed, 'O God, make the bad people good, and the good people nice.'"

—*What's So Amazing About Grace?*, PHILIP YANCEY

"I suddenly find I'm tired. Tired of fussing over your perpetually offended sense of the proprieties. Tired, as Saint Paul was, of having to come to you hat in hand and explain for the thousandth time that the jailhouse door is really open. And tired above all of having to apologize for God because he doesn't run what you consider a respectable penitentiary."

—*Between Noon and Three, Romance, Law and the Outrage of Grace*, ROBERT FARRAR CAPON

O NE SUNDAY MORNING a community of ducks waddled off to the First Duck Church to hear their duck preacher. The ducks had always "done" church in a particular way, they were comfortable with their status quo religion. What the ducks did not realize was that even though they had been told their church was a Christian church, they had also always been taught that how they walked (waddled) and talked (quacked) was the basis of their salvation and faith.

They had always kept to themselves and were suspicious of other fowl, and they rejected those who had anything to do with "outsiders." They felt that they were better Christians than chickens (and geese for that matter) because of their longstanding special beliefs and practices.

One of the most unique proofs that they felt set them apart—and made them better Christians than chickens and geese—was their distinctive waddle and their unique quack.

Some of the bolder ducks actually said what others only dared to think. They dogmatically claimed to be the one and only true Christians because of their waddle and quack. Their usual Sunday fare was one of two themes:

1. How much better they were than ducks in other fowl churches.
2. How God was not happy with many of them, because were slipping in their devotion to the rules and regulations of First Duck, and consequently they needed to "get right or get left."

But this Sunday was like no other Sunday. This Sunday they heard the pure, authentic, and unadulterated gospel of Jesus Christ. The duck preacher gave an inspirational and eloquent sermon about God's grace—about how, because of God's grace, the ducks would no longer have to live the way they lived. The duck preacher spoke eloquently from Galatians, but he also quoted Isaiah 40:28–31, explaining that God, by his grace, had given the ducks wings with which to fly—they would no longer have to waddle.

Do you not know? Have you not heard? The Lord is the everlasting God, the Creator of the ends of the earth. He will not grow tired or weary, and his understanding no one can fathom. He gives strength to the weary and increases the power of the weak. Even youths grow tired and weary, and young men stumble and fall; but those who hope in the Lord will renew their strength. They will soar on wings like eagles; they will run and not grow weary, they will walk and not be faint. (Isaiah 40:28–31)

The sermon was so inspiring and the preacher was so convincing that a few quacks of "a-men" reverberated throughout the duck congregation before those who responded had a chance to really think about how the message of the sermon might change their lives.

After the service was over many of the ducks discussed the sermon in front of the church. After intense conversations most of them decided that there was no way that they would start flying like geese. After all, many emotionally quacked, their families had waddled for years, and it was what they had always done. They wanted to be different. It made them feel special.

They bristled at the suggestion that their duck waddle would be discarded and left behind in favor of grace and soaring on wings like eagles. So the duck preacher's sermon that proclaimed the gospel of Jesus Christ was—well, it was like water off of a duck's back. Most of the congregation rejected the gospel that day and waddled back home.

All too often we waddle into church, and then we waddle back into our lives, unchallenged and unchanged. If we attend a Christ-centered church, we will hear about the gospel and about grace. We hear that God will give us what we lack, that he will fill us with his goodness and his love. . . . but then, perhaps because we are creatures (or ducks) of habit, we simply waddle back to our comfortable ritualistic deeds and habits.

I know about the duck walk—I did it for over 35 years. I waddled because it was what I was taught—and what I came to believe. I was trapped in an unholy huddle of legalism and man-made religion, convinced that the vast majority of people who said they were Christians were deceived. I was convinced that God wanted me to suck it up, have courage, obey, overcome, do-do-do and eventually, somehow, barely "make it."

GOOD NEWS IS NOT ALWAYS WELCOME

One would think that the announcement of God's grace, the best news that anyone could ever hear, would always be welcomed. It sounds like a no-brainer. Here's salvation—it's free, by God's grace—all you have to do is accept that Jesus Christ alone can give you what you can never accomplish on your own. But that last part—that's the kicker that many people can't deal with. It means that our denominational distinctives and traditions that we often confuse with the core gospel have no part in our salvation. It means that what we have always believed about redemption and justification might even be wrong, and more than that—our much-loved distinctives, if they receive undue emphasis and become a priority, may actually be an enemy of grace.

> **[Grace] means that our denominational distinctives and traditions that we often confuse with the core gospel have no part in our salvation.**

Grace is more often than not rejected, at least initially. When grace is announced, humans do not normally respond with big parades and parties. It's exactly what happened when Jesus, grace personified, came into our world.

The Great I AM did not come from outside of time and space, from eternity, to validate and reinforce religious legalism. Jesus, the second person of the Trinity, the eternal Son of God entered into our time-bound, limited, and corrupted world to save us from religion, not to give us another one.

The birth of Jesus signaled something new, dramatic, and earth-shaking. Because we were beyond hope, because our sins had separated us from God, because we were hopelessly lost—God came to find us. We were trapped by endless rituals and in bondage to legalistic traditions. We needed help (and we still do!)

This is one of the great truths of biblical Christianity. All other world religions teach that the goal in life for humans is to struggle, endure, search—and by our efforts find God. Once we find him all religions teach that it is imperative for us to please God, and to appease him—by our works. The truth is that God has come to find us and offer us grace, in spite of whom we are and what we have done.

A few years ago I was driving home, listening to a Christian radio station. I became upset with the hypercritical ranting and raving I was hearing. The preacher sounded too much like what I used to sound like—too much like Greg Albrecht without Jesus. He scared me, or maybe it was my past that scared me. I hit the scan button.

At first I thought I was listening to a golden oldies station that played blasts from the past—from a time when I was young and had all the time in the world to memorize the lyrics to top-40 songs. But after listening for a minute, I realized that this was an updated version of one of the songs of my youth.

For the first time I carefully considered the lyrics now being sung by Pearl Jam. The song tells a story about two young people out on a date, their car crashes and the young man's sweetheart is killed. The young man is heartbroken and wails during the chorus:

> Where oh where can my baby be
> The Lord took her away from me
> She's gone to heaven so *I've got to be good*
> *So I can see my baby when I leave this world.*
> (emphasis added)

Many believers who go to church faithfully, who read their Bibles and pray on a regular basis, would see no difficulty with the implications of these words. But these lyrics do not accurately reflect what the Bible tells us. Being good does not ensure our acceptance into God's kingdom of heaven.

Many surveys have found that a majority of church-going Christians believe that "God helps those who help themselves" is a verse in the Bible. More importantly, most believe the principle of God helping those who help themselves defines who and what God is and the relationship he offers us. The truth is just the opposite. Those who realize that they cannot help themselves and cannot earn their own salvation accept Jesus Christ as sufficient to do what they can never do.

So, with apologies to these lyrics depicting the pain of lost adolescent love, salvation and entering God's kingdom of heaven isn't a matter of "I've got to be good so I can see my baby when I leave this world."

The criteria as to whether we will "see our baby when we leave this world" is not our good works—if it is, we are all lost. Our baby won't be there and neither will we. The criteria is this: God's grace is sufficient.

Salvation is a matter that God has been and is good, holy and righteous. The gospel of grace tells us that God's goodness is good enough and sufficient. We should believe, as Isaiah says

> . . . those who hope in the Lord will renew their strength.
> They will soar on wings like eagles.
>
> —ISAIAH 40:31

If we believe that God is good enough, then we don't have to waddle around any more, God will enable us to fly. But no amount of flapping our wings will make us fly—that's something only God can do. When we accept Jesus Christ as sufficient for our salvation, we repent of trying to do it ourselves, and we acknowledge that our salvation is not a combination of what we do plus what Jesus does.

YOUR DEBT HAS BEEN PAID— EVEN THOUGH IT DOESN'T SEEM TO ADD UP

Grace doesn't make sense. Grace doesn't add up. Why would Jesus come to be one of us, to pay a debt he did not owe, because we owed a debt we could not pay? Why would he pay for our sins in advance, before we were even alive to commit them? Why would he do that? Free? No strings? What was in it for him? What if we take advantage of his willingness to forgive us every time we sin? What if we take advantage of God's unconditional love? Surely there is some point when God's patience and grace ends, and when we become toast and chopped liver.

Remember the parable of the unforgiving debtor in Matthew 18:21–35? Jesus gave this parable to explain the magnitude of God's grace, and that his grace has no limitations or conditions. Act one of the parable paints the story of a financial manager who finds that he owes his employer a staggering amount of money, perhaps as much as the annual revenue of a small nation or city-state.

Jesus does not tell us why the manager had come to owe this prodigious sum of money. Perhaps Jesus didn't want us to get lost in obsessing over the sleazy sins that resulted in the manager's debt. How the debt added up is not the point of this parable. The point of the parable is that the manager's debt is far beyond his resources or that of his family ever to repay. When he stood before his employer for an accounting, the manager heard the verdict that his entire family and all of his possessions would have to be sold to begin to repay the debt.

The financial manager threw himself on the mercy of his employer, begging for time so that he could repay his debt. His employer responded with something the indebted manager would never have dreamed of, and certainly would not have asked for. His debt was being canceled. All of it! No strings. No conditions.

- The debt that we owe God is so enormous that there is no human way we can settle the account. Our situation is hopeless. We are powerless to repay our debt. There is no human act or combination of actions—deeds, virtues, efforts, good works—that can pay the bill.

- When the debtor throws himself upon the mercy of the King, and not before, he is forgiven. Only when we accept our inability to save ourselves and express our complete faith and belief in Jesus Christ to do for us what neither we nor religion can ever do, then our debt is paid. However, as long as religion convinces us that we can waddle along somehow taking care of our own bills, our debt remains unpaid.

- When Jesus said, on the cross, "It is finished"—he meant, "the debt is paid." He has done what we can never do.

But now the parable gets ugly and personal—after grace, then what? After grace, how should we then live? Act two of the parable depicts the manager who was forgiven, redeemed, and reconciled— the same man who was rescued, saved, and freed from his debt— going out and refusing to forgive one of his debtors.

Fresh from the riches of God's grace just given to him, he goes out and meets a peer. His contemporary owes him a meager amount compared to the staggering debt the manager had just been forgiven. According to the parable, the newly forgiven man grabs that person by the neck and screams at him, "Pay me what you owe me."

And as we read this part of the parable, we protest, "Oh no, that can't be! How can this man act that way?"

And that's one of the morals of this parable—if we realize we have been forgiven, we will be forgiving, even if it takes some painful experiences to help us understand that we cannot be anything but forgiving.

Who are we, the forgiven, to do anything but forgive? Our mission is to tell others about God's amazing grace. Our calling is to share the unbelievably good news that God's grace is good enough and sufficient for our salvation. We have the precious opportunity of telling others that God is looking for them and that God will forgive them once they fall at his feet and ask for his grace.

God's grace calls us to be his tools, instruments of his peace. God's grace invites us to fly, placing our hope and confidence in God, leaving our religious quacks and waddles behind. God's grace leads us to display and reflect (not produce, for we cannot produce God's grace) grace to others so that others may see Jesus through what he is doing in our lives.

CHAPTER TEN—REVIEW AND RECAP

The duck walk. What we have always done and what we have always believed is comfortable. Being grace-based and Christ-centered calls for reformation and change that can be like water off a duck's back.

God helps those who help themselves? The truth is just the opposite—God helps those who recognize they cannot help themselves and trust in him to do what they can never accomplish.

Being good so we can see our loved ones in heaven. Being good is not the criteria used for admission into God's kingdom of heaven.

Infinite debt. We owe God a debt that is too enormous for us ever to pay. Based on our humanly produced spiritual resources, we are bankrupt and without hope.

The installment plan. *Bad News Religion* tries to convince us that we can pay for our own way, or at the very least, make a contribution to our salvation.

Bought and paid for. Jesus paid a debt he did not owe because we owed a debt we could not pay.

11

The Price of Legalism

"Obsession with spiritual success can take you on idiotic detours. . . . I know a man who needs to be good so badly that he cannot face up to the puniest fault. He often groans about being a poor, poor sinner— always in gorgeous generalities and always as a trick to get people to reassure him of his unusual virtue. But when his wife complains that he forgot to take out the garbage, he is ready to hire a criminal lawyer to defend himself against her indictment."

—*Forgive and Forget—Healing the Hurts We Don't Deserve,*
Lewis Smedes

"The gospel of grace is the end of religion, the final posting of the CLOSED sign on the sweatshop of the human race's perpetual struggle to think well of itself. For that, at bottom, is what religion is: the human species' well-meant but dim-witted attempt to gain approval of its unapprovable condition by doing odd jobs it thinks some important Something will thank it for. . . . You won't learn anything positive about religion from Christianity and if you look for Christianity in religion, you'll never find it."

—*Between Noon and Three, Romance, Law and the Outrage of
Grace,* Robert Farrar Capon

Years ago an old woman was found dead in her home in a North American metropolitan area. She had lived a reclusive life and her home was a collection of junk and debris. She had isolated herself from almost all human contact. The evidence that she left behind revealed that she had allowed herself very little in the way of creature comforts. Yet, in the middle of all that junk and debris, authorities found bankbooks and stock portfolios totaling in the millions of dollars. She could have lived like a queen, enjoying the best life had to offer, but instead, she lived a miserable existence.

You may read about this story and shake your head in amazement, but there are millions of people who live this same kind of existence spiritually. They live a life of spiritual poverty. Their lives are filled with religious rituals and regulations, and they are busy with religious activities—but in spite of all their religion, their relationships with God are distant and impersonal.

Does your faith consist of rules and regulations, but lack a deep love and passion for God? Is what you know as Christianity more of a burden than a joy? Is your life as a Christian filled with slave-like devotion to religious activities? You may be paying the price of religious legalism.

In Luke 7:36–50 we read of Jesus being invited to a dinner by a man named Simon. Simon was an extremely religious man, a Pharisee, a religious ruler, a teacher of the law. Simon invited many of his friends who we can be sure were much like Simon—religious, righteous, and moral. They were all surprised with another guest who was not part of their religious clique, someone who made them all severely uncomfortable.

In the days of Jesus, when someone gave a dinner party, people who were not invited guests were allowed to visit and sit in the courtyard to observe and listen. Dinners and gatherings at this time were occasions when conversation and discussions centered on important moral and spiritual issues—and many who were not invited to dine were interested in hearing what the guests, and particularly the guest of honor, had to say. It was a little bit like talk radio in the United States today—people tuned in to listen.

And, like some talk radio, there were times when visitors who were not invited dinner guests were invited to speak with and question those who were at the dinner. This custom allowed someone to enter Simon's home who Simon would otherwise never have had any contact with. We aren't told her name; she is simply described as a "sinful woman."

They were total opposites, Simon and this sinful woman. She was a woman with a public reputation for an immoral lifestyle. He was a man with a public reputation for high moral values. They had nothing, it would seem, in common.

He was obviously devoutly religious; she certainly didn't seem to be. Yet, one evening, God brought this spiritual odd couple together, because he wanted

Their lives are filled with religious rituals and regulations, and they are busy with religious activities—but in spite of all their religion, their relationship with God is distant and impersonal.

to teach Simon something he could never learn any other way.

Luke tells us that when this sinful woman, obviously someone who would never be invited to Simon's table, learned that Jesus was to be at Simon's house, she purchased an extremely expensive alabaster jar of perfume and came to the dinner to be one of the uninvited guests. The sinful woman must have known that her presence would not be welcome, but she went to see Jesus anyway.

As Jesus was eating and talking with Simon and his guests, he did so in the custom of the day, reclining on his side and eating. At some point this sinful woman left the courtyard area, and without an invitation, walked up and sat down at Jesus' feet, obviously attracting the attention of everyone in the group, and began to cry. The Bible doesn't say what she said—if anything. No explanations, no reasons, she just started to cry.

This intrusion and outburst of emotion by the unwelcome, uninvited guest must have caused all conversation to cease. We can imagine that the only sound was the woman's sobs, as she had adopted a posture of sitting at Jesus' feet—to do so was considered a sign of total humility. Her tears began to fall upon Jesus' feet and as they did she undid her hair and let it fall, which was a scandal in itself.

Respectable women were not supposed to let down their hair in public. With Jesus' feet wet with her tears, she took her hair and began to wash them. Then she broke the vial of perfume, pouring it upon his feet and continued to wipe them with her hair.

Simon and his guests must have been beside themselves—they were scandalized by this act of worship from a well-known, publicly acknowledged sinner. Luke reminds us:

> When the Pharisee [Simon] who had invited him [Jesus] saw this, he said to himself, "If this man were a prophet, he would know who is touching him and what kind of woman she is—that she is a sinner!"
>
> —LUKE 7:39

In Simon's mind, Jesus had just forfeited all of his credentials as a prophet, teacher, and moral authority. Jesus had allowed someone whom religion defined as morally unclean to touch him, something a good Pharisee would never have allowed. This would make Jesus himself morally suspect in their eyes. Little did Simon know that Jesus knew exactly what he was thinking.

Luke tells us that just as Simon was thinking these thoughts, Jesus told him a story. The story concerned two men who both owed money to a certain lender. One man owed the lender 500 denarii, the equivalent of almost two years' salary. The other man owed the lender 50 denarii, about two month's worth of salary. Neither of them, Jesus told Simon, had the ability to pay the lender.

The lender showed mercy and forgave both of their debts. Jesus then asked Simon which of the two men Simon thought would love the lender more. Simon replied, "I suppose the one who had the bigger debt canceled." Jesus answered, "You have judged correctly, Simon."

Then Jesus turned Simon's attention to the sinful woman at his feet and said to Simon,

> Do you see this woman? I came into your house. You did not give me any water for my feet, but she wet my feet with her tears and wiped them with her hair. You did not give me a kiss, but this woman, from the time I entered, has not stopped kissing my feet. You did not put oil on my head, but she has poured perfume on my feet. Therefore, I tell you, her many sins have been forgiven—for she loved much. But he who has been forgiven little loves little.
>
> —LUKE 7:44–47

Simon wasn't the first to be trapped by the snare of spiritual elitism, and he wasn't the last. Many of us feel spiritually safe and secure because we are involved in religious activity. Religious activity, especially the kind that has us busy with keeping rules and regulations, is a fertile breeding ground for legalism.

Legalism, as Jesus points out so dramatically to Simon, results in four deadly traps for those caught in it.

1) Legalism Will Blind Us to Our True Condition

Jesus told Simon that the amount of sin in a person's life isn't the important issue; the awareness of sin is. Simon, feeling comfortable at his success in keeping God's law, had never asked himself a very important question, one Jesus was trying to get him to think about. The question is: How much sin does it take for a person to be considered a sinner?

In Jesus' parable he described two men in debt. One owed a huge sum, the other owed a smaller sum, but what they both had in common was that neither of them was able to pay off the debt. If you don't have the ability to pay the debt, it doesn't matter if you owe 10 dollars or 10 million dollars.

Picture two men running toward the edge of the Grand Canyon as fast as they can. Their goal is to jump over the huge canyon and reach the other side. One of these two men is a college athlete, the best long jumper in the country. He won the Olympic gold medal for the long jump. No one in the world can jump as far as he can.

The other man is an overweight, out-of-shape businessman, huffing and puffing for all he's worth. Let's imagine that they both jump at precisely the same time. The college athlete launches his perfectly toned body—and sails, breaking all the records for distance ever set. But after he sails to the world record he starts to sink to the bottom of the Grand Canyon. As good as he is, he isn't good enough to jump across the Grand Canyon. The businessman, on the other hand, jumps for all he is worth, goes a few feet, and immediately begins to drop like a rock.

It would be silly for the athlete, in midair, to snub his nose at the businessman, saying, "Look how well I jumped, and how badly you jumped. I'm obviously a much better jumper than you are." While the athlete indeed jumped much further than the businessman, he was still far short of the goal. The goal wasn't to jump as far as you could; the goal was to reach the other side. Both fail and both have the same bone-shattering conclusion to their jump waiting for them at the bottom of the Grand Canyon.

This is what Simon didn't get. Legalism is pride in the pitiful spiritual distance we can jump, the moral accomplishments, and character we can produce. Legalism is self-righteousness. Simon couldn't see that he and the sinful woman were in the same situation—both headed to the bottom of the Grand Canyon. Simon may have appeared to be by far a morally superior person—but he was a sinner just like the sinful woman.

Bad News Religion blinds us to our true condition. It deceives us into thinking that our good works and religious activity make us acceptable to God—and as a result we feel comfortable, safe, and secure. We don't feel any need for God's grace and mercy. In fact, those who are trapped by legalism are often unaware that they desperately need God's grace, and therefore, they snub God's grace.

To those who work hard to perfect themselves and are proud of their religious accomplishments, grace is an excuse for people who are not really trying. After all, *Bad News Religion* leads us to conclude, if people really worked hard enough, they wouldn't need to hope for God's free handouts of grace. Legalism fools us into thinking that we are doing all that is needed to be done. We don't need God's welfare programs.

If you are a slave of *Bad News Religion,* you may perceive your relationship with God to be somewhat like a business arrangement. You might feel that God owes you his favor because you have kept all, or at least most, of his rules. When you go into a store and find something you want to buy and purchase it, you don't feel any debt of gratitude to the person who sold it to you, do you? They were doing you no favors. You paid the price asked for the item and therefore feel entitled to receive what you paid for.

But, on the other hand, if you are destitute, homeless, and broke—and someone gives you something you could never afford, or ever pay back, you will feel totally different towards him. He is giving you something you can't buy or pay for. It is an act of grace.

When our faith is reduced to merely keeping rules and regulations, we are robbed of any true joy. Of course, following Jesus Christ and obeying him is not wrong. Obedience is what Christ produces in those who God has saved by his grace. God wants us to realize that our feeble attempts at doing good works cannot earn our salvation. Eternal life and forgiveness is a gift from God—not a reward for living a good life.

2) LEGALISM WILL DISGUISE OUR REAL NEED FOR GOD

As we have considered Simon and the sinful woman you may have identified more with how the sinful woman felt than with Simon. You may feel far away from God. Like this sinful woman, you know you are a sinner. And though you know you have failed God, you desperately want to have a good relationship with him. You want to believe that he loves you. You long to be able to experience God's forgiveness, grace, and cleansing, but you feel that you are unworthy.

If that's how you feel, then the words of Jesus will water your thirsty soul just as they did the sinful woman's. Jesus told her, as he tells all of us,

> Come to me, all you who are weary and burdened, and I will give you rest.
>
> —MATTHEW 11:28

From believing that God only waited to judge her for her many failures, the sinful woman suddenly realized that God was waiting instead to forgive and accept her. Simon had the exact same need for God's forgiveness that the sinful woman did. Remember, Simon was scheduled to arrive at the bottom of the Grand Canyon at about the same time she was—but legalism disguised Simon's need of God.

The sinful woman's vision was not obscured by pride and self-righteousness, and as a result she was able to see her need more clearly. That's why she had come to see Jesus. That's why she was kissing his feet and washing them with her hair.

But what a contrast when Simon approached Jesus—Simon was aloof, smug, conceited, and proud—he was cool and detached with Jesus. Simon had, of course, invited Jesus to dinner, but his real agenda may have been to check Jesus out, to engage him in some theological and intellectual games and to match wits with him.

It was customary in those days for the host to wash his guests' feet. Dust would gather on their sandals and the host would courteously wash the dust off. Guests were welcomed with a kiss, which was a common greeting. And finally the guest's head was customarily anointed with oil, usually sweet smelling oil for refreshing.

Yet, as Jesus pointed out, Simon had performed none of these common courtesies for him. It was a visible example of Simon's detached distance from God. Jesus is making it clear that spiritual pride had disguised Simon's need for God and caused him to feel equal to, or perhaps even superior to, this young preacher from Galilee. Since Simon did not feel a great need for forgiveness, he loved little. *Bad News Religion* disguised his real need for God.

But this woman whose very life repulsed Simon, had washed Jesus' feet with her tears, the feet Simon would not touch. She had kissed the feet of Jesus repeatedly in humility, while Simon would not lower himself to welcome Jesus with a common kiss on the cheek. And while Simon would not offer Jesus even an inexpensive oil for refreshing, she had spent lavishly on a very expensive perfume that she poured not on his head, but upon his feet.

Simon's sins were less visible; they were pride, arrogance, hypocrisy, and self-righteousness. The woman's sins, on the other hand, were visible, public, and well known—perhaps a matter of public record. But there is no difference in God's eyes. Simon's self-righteousness clouded his ability to see his real need for God. Legalism had robbed him of the intimacy and closeness that comes with understanding God's love and his mercy.

Are you enslaved to regulations and rules that have seduced and blinded you, robbing you of the joy God wants to give his children? Christ-centered Christianity brings joy; legalism brings drudgery. Jesus sets us free; *Bad News Religion* enslaves us. If you are burdened by trying to keep all the rules and regulations of religion, Jesus offers you rest. Neither Simon nor the sinful woman, even though they were total opposites, had real peace with God in the beginning. But the sinful woman was willing to recognize that she was a sinner in need of a Savior while Simon wasn't. You may be like Simon, devoutly religious but trapped in the form of religion, or you may be like the sinful woman. Jesus' offer is the same to both. "Come unto me, and I will give you rest."

You may have heard the story about the priest, who had only just arrived in New York City and was assigned to work in a high crime area, populated by the homeless, drug addicts and pushers, along with criminals of every description. One night the priest was walking home when suddenly he felt a gun in his ribs. Then he heard a raspy voice: "All right mister, gimme all your money!" The priest quickly reached for his wallet and, as he did, the would-be thief noticed the priest's clerical clothing.

The thief was immediately overcome with shame. He said,

"Forgive me, Father. I didn't know you were a priest." The priest was a little shaken, but nevertheless replied, "That's all right, my son. Just repent of your sin. Here, have a cigar." The thief replied, "Oh, no, thank you, Father, I don't smoke during Lent."

It is easy to become a spiritual impostor. It doesn't take long to learn the accepted external rituals that are prescribed and begin to faithfully observe them. We can behave like a Christian—we can walk and talk like a Christian, and many (if not most) people will assume that we are Christians. We can be in the right place at the right time wearing the right clothes saying and doing the right things—but does that make us a Christian?

3) Legalism Will Breed Arrogance Rather Than Sincerity

Many of us, even with the best of intentions, can, in very short order, become spiritual impostors and hypocrites. We learn how to fake it. In Matthew 15:1–20 we read the story of Jesus sparring with some of the greatest spiritual hypocrites who ever lived. The Pharisees were leaders and teachers of the Jewish law. Though many of them were no doubt sincere and devout, some were not. They were spiritual imposters who had grown extremely sophisticated at faking their spirituality.

One day the Pharisees came to Jesus to question him. They confronted him about why his disciples did not wash their hands before they ate. You have to understand that the Pharisees weren't referring to the normal practice of washing dirty hands before eating—they were talking about a ritual engaged in solely for religious reasons—a ritual cleansing. The Pharisees, over the years, had taken the law of God given through Moses and added "clarifications" to it.

You see, the law of God was not enough for them—they had to

improve it—just like some today who call themselves Christians. They have to improve Jesus. Jesus Christ, they argue, is a good start—of course his cross has meaning for us. BUT—they say, we are not saved by what he did alone—we are also saved by what we do.

Salvation, for them, is not what the Bible says. The Bible says we are saved only by grace, only by what Christ did for us. Period. Nothing more. But people who are enslaved by legalism say that we are saved by what Christ did PLUS what we do. They are modern-day Pharisees. The Pharisees of Jesus' day did the same with the old covenant. Over time they "improved" God's law with their additions and modifications. In time, what they added took on a life of its own, actually becoming more authoritative in the eyes of many than the law of God itself.

The problem was that in many cases, the tradition of the elders, originally designed to clarify and explain the law, went far beyond what the law originally demanded. In many cases it ultimately failed to do justice to the law at all. While there were limited occasions in the Old Testament when God prescribed cleansing and hand rinsing for priests and even on rare occasions for all the people (Exodus 19:10; Leviticus 16:26,28; Numbers 19:7,8, 19; Leviticus 15:11; Deuteronomy 21:6), nowhere in the law was ritual hand rinsing prescribed for everyone and in connection with every meal. But the Pharisees had now taken this issue and made it a major point of spirituality. They had begun majoring on minor issues and minoring on major issues.

When the Pharisees asked Jesus why his disciples did not wash their hands for spiritual reasons before they ate a meal—well, in short, they were asking Jesus why his disciples were not following man-made religious additions to God's law. Jesus responded by asking the Pharisees why they broke the command of God for the sake of their tradition (v.3). Then he quoted the law, which demanded that children honor their parents. This clear law to honor one's parents—one of the commandments—had been nullified by what was called the tradition of the elders—one of the things that had been added to God's law by human beings. What was this addition?

The Pharisees taught that there was a way around what some considered a financial burden—caring for their needy and elderly parents. When a parent asked an adult child for help, or for something that they needed, the adult child could tell their parent that the requested item was off limits, because they had dedicated that resource to God as a gift or offering. This man-made teaching enabled adult children to deny much needed help and assistance to their parents. Ironically, this act did not mean the children had to actually give a monetary gift or resource to the Temple or the priests; they could still keep it for their own use.

Here was a loophole—a clever way of allowing people to get around doing what they should do, and what God's law directed them to do—to honor their parents. At the same time this little loophole allowed people the satisfaction of keeping their resources for themselves while being smug about obeying the law.

In Matthew 15 we see that the Pharisees actually felt superior to Jesus' disciples because they involved themselves in ritual rinsing of their hands before they ate while Jesus' disciples did not. But, while their goal was to arrogantly expose what they felt was Jesus' lack of spirituality, Jesus turned the tables on them, exposing them as spiritual imposters.

The Pharisees were terribly offended by Jesus' statements. How dare he question their motives? Legalism breeds arrogance rather than sincerity. We can begin to feel, because we are observing the external rituals of religion, that we are spiritually superior to those who don't do the things we do—and that no one has the right to question us about the true condition of our hearts.

Performance-based religion leads us to feel arrogant and superior about our spirituality as the Pharisees did, bypassing the more important issue of sincerity. The truth is that we can perform religious rituals without sincerity. But we can't fool God. Any attempt to fake spirituality before God will always fail. We might fool other humans, but we don't fool God, and in the end we are only fooling ourselves.

But while we can't fool God, the truth is that we can fool other human beings. Sometimes when we "fake" our spirituality, we can find others beginning to treat us as spiritually mature, or very religious. We can get caught up in religious pretense. When we perform some external religious ritual or parrot religious phrases in our prayers that do not really reflect the attitudes of our heart, we are merely being legalistic. We are faking it.

Sometimes we feel that we must say religious phrases or speak to God in just the right way with just the right words, or he will not hear us. Some believe that God will only listen when we say a magic phrase, almost like a mantra, or when we use a specific formula, or when we say exactly the right things—some people call it a prayer of positive confession. Some believe God is obligated to hear us if we use the right combinations of consonants and vowels. Others say that one of the best ways to reach God is by endlessly repeating certain prayers—even the Lord's Prayer.

But God is far less interested with our words than he is with our heart. Our heart is what God is focused on, not our religious activity or words. When the Pharisees tried to look good on the outside, they felt God would be impressed with their attempts at self-improvement.

But God isn't interested in our self-improvement—he wants to transform us. And he alone can transform us. He wants to make something brand new out of us, not just redecorate or remodel us. He is not interested in patching us up with band-aids—instead he offers us a new life.

The end result of legalism can be illustrated by the story of the little girl who went to dinner at the home of her first grade friend. The vegetable was buttered broccoli, and the mother asked if she liked it. The little girl had been carefully trained by her parents to be gracious, and to be a good guest, so she politely replied, "Oh yes, I love broccoli." But when the bowl of broccoli was passed to her she declined to take any. The hostess said, "I thought you loved broccoli." The girl replied very sweetly, "Oh yes, ma'am. I do. But not enough to eat it."

We can say we love God; we can parrot religious phrases and be involved in any number of religious rituals. We can even develop a religious reputation, one we highly value. We can be so convinced of our own spirituality that we can look down on those who do not "appear" as religious as we do. We can be in the right place at the right time wearing the right clothing saying and doing the right things—the Pharisees did that. But their legalism bred arrogance rather than sincerity.

4) LEGALISM WILL LEAD US TO DO GOOD THINGS FOR THE WRONG REASONS

Legalism can lead us to become paranoid about religious appearances. For legalists, how others perceive them can become far more important than their true spiritual condition.

Pharisees, both past and present, can become more concerned with how they look to others than how they look to God. They become spiritual imposters. Spiritual imposters do good things for the wrong reasons. Soon religious activity is primarily for the purpose of keeping up appearances especially to impress those who follow the same list of dos and don'ts. We can become extremely concerned about what people see us do, and not do. The result is that doing good things can become nothing more than spiritual makeup, designed to cover our true spiritual blemishes.

Bad News Religion is a spiritual cosmetic industry—with the main concern being what others see, and don't see, when they look at us. When women go to the powder room they will often say that they are going to "put on their face." Cosmetics help us with our physical appearance. Spiritual cosmetics put on a spiritual face.

Legalism is the "foundation" of spiritual cosmetics. It compels us to put on an act to impress others who themselves are putting on an act to impress us. The act we put on may be good—the actions and behaviors may be good things to do, but we are doing them for the wrong reason—and in the process we become spiritual imposters.

To be engaged in good deeds of any kind, to be involved in religious activity of any kind simply to improve your reputation, or make people think you are spiritual is hypocrisy. God is not pleased or appeased when we do good things for wrong reasons.

Bad News Religion is feel-good religion and look-good religion. But it never even scratches the surface of our deepest need, which is to know, and to find peace with the God who made us.

Legalism is part of the human condition. It's a spiritual virus that threatens all of us. We're all guilty of masking our deficiencies and hyping our resumes. But the greatest deception we ever perpetrate is self-deception.

While the truth may not be easy to swallow, Jesus said the truth could set us free. In Christ we can be free to seek forgiveness, free to receive acceptance, free to accept the truth about ourselves, because we know that no matter how bad the truth may be, God loves us anyway.

You don't have to be perfect for God to love you. God loves you, not because you are lovable, but because it is his nature to love you. He wants to free you from slavery to religious appearances, self-deception, and lies that are designed to cover up the real truth. He wants to free you from the terrible burden of trying to keep up a religious facade. God offers you and me a chance to get real—and to stop being spiritual imposters.

Chapter Eleven—Review and Recap

Bad News Religion enslaves us, with four deadly traps:

1) **It blinds us to our true condition.** *Bad News Religion* redefines our relationship with God as a business arrangement or contract. We will begin to feel that God owes us his favor because of what we have accomplished.

2) **It disguises our real need for God.** Legalism seduces us into thinking that we do not need God. We can believe that if we are in the right place at the right time wearing the right clothes and doing the right things God is pleased with us.

3) **It breeds arrogance rather than sincerity.** We are encouraged to compare ourselves with others to make ourselves feel better about ourselves and in the process become arrogant hypocrites. God is not interested in our pitiful attempts at self-improvement. He doesn't want to merely remodel us and patch us up with band-aids, he wants to transform us.

4) **It leads us to do good things for the wrong reasons.** Legalism leads us to focus on appearances, doing good deeds to look good. *Bad News Religion* is a spiritual cosmetics industry, helping us to "put on our face" so that others will be impressed with what they see.

12

Jesus is the Answer

"A knowing Church has replaced a believing Church, a possessing Church has replaced a needy Church, total authority has replaced obedience. Not in theory or principle, perhaps, but in fact and in reality. It has become its own mistress and no longer needs a master. . . . its all too human directives are given out as the directives of Christ; human commandments are turned into divine commandments. Such a Church is a caricature of itself."

—*The Church,* HANS KUNG

"The visible church is all the people who get together from time to time in God's name. Anybody can find out who they are by going to look. The invisible church is all the people God uses for his hands and feet in this world. Nobody can find out who they are except God. Think of them as two circles. The optimist says they are concentric. The cynic says they don't even touch. The realist says they occasionally overlap."

—*Wishful Thinking,* FREDERICK BUECHNER

TENS OF MILLIONS OF PEOPLE toil under the impression that the God of Christianity is mad and can't wait for an opportunity to punish them. You may know someone who has given up on God. You may be that someone. You may be burned out because you've been through an earthly version of hell that called itself a church, but was nothing more than legalistic religion. What you need to know is that God is not at all what, who, or like what you have been taught or shown.

So by all means get out of *Bad News Religion,* but don't give up on God and the authentic Christianity he offers to you. God loves you, whether you like it or not. God loves you, whether you believe it or not. If you haven't accepted God's love yet, God still loves you.

Bad News Religion is to blame for the spiritual confusion and disorientation many in North America and Europe now experience. Many who were "born into" Christianity and "grew up" in a Christian culture are disenchanted. They have had horrible experiences with legalism, enduring spiritual slavery in the name of God, and have written off all of Christianity as a result.

Researchers call them seekers and searchers, and in many cases they are customizing their own spiritual realities. Many browse through Christian churches and religion in general, picking and choosing portions as they would in a self-serve cafeteria, blending differing, and often contradictory, views to fit what they feel they need. Call it "do-it-yourself" religion, "mix and match" spirituality or "cut and paste" faith; the emphasis is on meeting subjectively determined needs.

This smorgasbord approach to faith and God is largely a result of profound dissatisfaction with the slavery and control of *Bad News Religion.* Disillusionment with performance-based religion is often manifested by a sweeping conclusion that the God of the Bible and all of Christianity is sick and perhaps even toxic.

Jumping from one ditch to another is a normal and historically documented human reaction—but being in a ditch is a prerequisite before starting this cycle. The primary reason many former Christians and would-be Christians are in a spiritual ditch is because legalism left them there.

Some are able to see that legalism is the problem. They have identified the problem, or at least the specific religious virus they have been exposed to, and the specific set of legalisms that enslaved them. They can see their dilemma, or at least what happened to them in the past. But as they pick and choose new religious ingredients and elements to fill the spiritual void in their lives they are often jumping out of one ditch into another. The solution to the problem is not some modified version of the problem in another ditch. The solution is the One and Only Answer.

Jesus Meets The Grand Inquisitor

Other than the parables that Jesus gave, Fyodor Dostoevsky (1821–1881) is thought by many to be the greatest Christian story-teller of all time. In *The Brothers Karamazov* he tells the legend of *The Grand Inquisitor*.

In the story Jesus returns to earth, to the time of the inquisitions in Spain, healing the sick and comforting those who mourn. Dostoevsky pictures Jesus coming to the people of Spain who were afflicted and encumbered with religion just as much as the Jews to whom Jesus came in the first century. The story, or legend, relates how Jesus was received by organized religion, whether it was 1st century Judaism or 16th century religion posing as Christianity. It's a parable of the ongoing battle between religion and God's grace.

The day after nearly a hundred heretics have been burned alive in the town square Jesus is walking by the cathedral in Seville just as a funeral procession is leaving, bringing with it a little white coffin. The mother of the child who has just died appeals to Jesus to raise her little girl from the dead. Jesus does so.

Just at that moment the Grand Inquisitor passes through the crowd, coming to the doors of the cathedral. Dostoevsky describes him: "He is an old man, almost ninety, tall and erect, with a withered face and sunken eyes, in which there is still a gleam of light. He is not dressed in his gorgeous cardinal's robes, as he was the day before, when he was burning the enemies of the Roman church—at this moment he is wearing his coarse, old, monk's cassock."

The Grand Inquisitor orders his guards to take Jesus and throw him into the prison of the Holy Inquisition. Dostoevsky paints a picture of the war between religion and Jesus—between counterfeit and authentic Christianity. In so doing he sets the stage for a confrontation between the Grand Inquisitor, representing visible religion, and Jesus, who is the head of the visible and invisible body of Christ on earth.

Jesus Alone is the Answer to *Bad News Religion.*

The Grand Inquisitor visits Jesus in prison, and in a monologue explains how he once believed in the glorious grace of the gospel, but eventually came to agree with religion that the only way to control humans is to take away the freedom of God's grace. He tells Jesus that religion rules over the people in his name, and that religion will not allow Jesus to return. The Grand Inquisitor admits that he tried to follow Jesus in his youth, but as the years went by he concluded that Jesus' gospel was impractical. The masses will never follow Jesus, he says.

The Grand Inquisitor concludes that Jesus' return to earth is getting in the way of the mission of the church that bears his name, and that he will have to be burned as a heretic. Jesus does not audibly respond, but instead kisses the old man, who is so moved that he releases Jesus from the prison. Jesus always responds with grace.

The big issue for legalism is control. *Bad News Religion* has its grand inquisitors who seek to control you and your life. The grand inquisitors of religion will stop at nothing to control all of you—you, your family, your career, your money, your mind, your future—all of it!

Not only did legalism once control me, but it also convinced me that my job as a husband, a father, a pastor, a teacher, and a college administrator was to control others. I was enlisted as an inquisitor to make other people's lives just as miserable as my own. Of course, that's not what I thought I was doing, and inquisitor wasn't given to me as a title, but *Bad News Religion* convinced me that I was doing what God wanted me to do.

Legalism is so successful in keeping people under its thumb that many do not want to leave the religious swamp in which they exist. Dostoevsky has his Grand Inquisitor explaining to Jesus that humans are anxious to hand over their freedom and are easily persuaded into believing that true freedom comes through submission to human religious authority. He tells Jesus that the masses long to obey, and will sell their freedom for bread. For the Grand Inquisitor the humans he rules are his slaves.

Grand inquisitors still roam this earth, and continue, in Christ's name, to deceive and seduce the masses who gullibly believe their perversion and corruption of the gospel. The masses want to believe that they earn God's favor, and *Bad News Religion* is all too willing to manipulate this belief for its own profit.

Do You Really Want to be Healed?

Sadly, many people who are deceived by religious legalism become so dysfunctional and warped that they do not want to be free in Christ—they prefer the slavery of humanly imposed rules and restrictions. Study any charismatic, authoritarian religious, or civil leader and you will find that many who suffered under his iron fist adored him and followed him to the grave. Whether that person is Jim Jones, David Koresh, Joseph Stalin, Adolph Hitler, or Saddam Hussein, the story is always the same.

Some people are so beguiled and mesmerized by the cult and its leader that they simply cannot leave. They are comfortable. They like their status quo. They don't know any other world, other than the narrow and restricted prison cell of the ideology that controls them. They are addicted to the pills, potions, philosophies, and poisons of religious legalism. They are afraid of the world outside of their religious swamp, and often decline freedom in Christ in favor of the security of the cult.

I am convinced that's why Jesus asked the man who had been crippled for 38 years if he wanted to get well (John 5:6). At first glance we might ask, "What kind of question was that?"

Jesus knew that not everyone wants to get well. Many adjust to the twisted and contorted world in which they live. In some cases people have been born into weird and perverted worldviews and know nothing else. Some people have been spiritually crippled all their lives and know no other reality. They have been taught to fear and distrust everyone outside of their group, and they don't want to be released from the comfort of their closeted world.

When Jesus heals captives of *Bad News Religion,* their world changes dramatically. If the crippled man accepted Jesus' offer to heal him, he would have to find a new job. The crippled man would be able to walk, opening up a whole new world. His old world was known to him—it was spiritually comfortable. Most of his friends were probably in similar circumstances.

If Jesus healed him, the formerly crippled man would be faced with massive changes, and change is not something we humans like. We often accept the misery and pain of what we know instead of freedom in a world of the unknown. I have tried to convince people who are in a religious swamp that there is a better way, and his name is Jesus. I have tried to give them directions, draw them a map, and help them out of the swamps. After all, I was there, and Jesus rescued me. I know that Jesus is the answer to religion.

But even though they are oppressed many will refuse to even discuss the possibility that they are in a religious swamp. And there is absolutely no way that most will listen to or allow any discussion of fault on the part of the leader and authority figure whose teachings imprison them.

The answer to legalism is, of course, Jesus. Jesus can rescue anyone from any form of organized legalism and cultic, heretical teaching. Believe me, I know. Jesus transcends humanly imposed boundaries. Jesus can pass through walls, even church walls (John 20:26). The biblical emphasis on the church is not on a physical entity, but upon the spiritual body of which Christ is head. The Church has no life apart from its Head. Jesus doesn't need human organizations or incorporated legal entities, though he can work in and through them in spite of their legalism and religion. Jesus alone is the answer to *Bad News Religion*.

Don't Give Up on God— He Hasn't Given Up on You!

If you are being held captive by legalism, you need to turn to Jesus. You need a Savior! It may not be an easy journey to leave the religious swamp you are in. God didn't miraculously take the Hebrews out of Egypt and two weeks later place them in a promised land. They wandered for 40 years in the wilderness.

I thank God that he hasn't appointed any human being or group of human beings to determine the eternal destiny of the exploited and oppressed who have been trampled under foot by *Bad News*

Religion. Bad News Religion is a fear religion, and jealousy guards its claim of being capable of judging a human's eternal destiny. I am thankful that God's grace reveals beyond a shadow of a doubt that God alone is our judge, and that he has not appointed any special private religious investigators or grand inquisitors to help him. God's grace is sufficient. God's grace is all we need.

What's the answer to *Bad News Religion?* Because human beings have made such a mess out of misrepresenting God, should we all head for our own subjectively determined theological hills and find a cave where we can get away from all of the sin in the world? Should we all subjectively determine what we need by picking and choosing elements we like from a variety of religious traditions? Is it logical to conclude that since we have been burned by one religious tradition perhaps another set of religious legalisms will be the answer?

Don't let bad experiences sour you on God. Don't let human beings who have given God a bad name (and that would be all of us, at one time or another) cause you to decide that everything in God's name is corrupt and perverted. Don't give up on God because someone did a less than adequate job of representing him.

In early Christianity essential teaching was organized into creeds. These creeds teach biblically based doctrines of the historic and orthodox faith. Innovative, speculative, and esoteric teachings are outside of the creeds—they were then, and they still are. If, for example, you hear some individual or group claim that they have new truth, you can be assured that what they are talking about is outside of the teachings of the Bible and is neither new nor true. There is no new truth; there is essentially no new heresy. All of the modern teachings that are heretical and cultic are simply repackaged, modified, and customized from earlier versions.

The Apostle's Creed teaches the triune God. It is an early document, which was revised many times, and drafted into its present form about A.D. 700. It has three long sentences, which form individual paragraphs, each beginning with (1) I believe in God the Father, (2) I believe in Jesus Christ his only son and (3) I believe in the Spirit. The Apostle's Creed affirms that God is the creator of heaven and earth, that Jesus was born of the virgin Mary, that he was crucified, died, and was buried, that he ascended to heaven and that he will come again.

The Apostle's Creed also affirms the holy catholic church. Some Protestants go ballistic when they read this, because they confuse the word "catholic" with Roman Catholic. The Apostle's Creed simply affirms that there is a universal body of Christ, which no denomination completely represents by its membership.

A second major creed is called the Nicene Creed, primarily concerned with the person and work of Jesus Christ. The Nicene Creed is the final statement of the council of Nicea, convened in A.D. 324 to counter the heretical teachings of Arius, who was essentially teaching that Jesus was created by God the Father.

The Nicene Creed follows the same Trinitarian formula as the Apostle's Creed with three long paragraphs about the Father, Son and Holy Spirit respectively. This creed insists that Jesus Christ is "true God from true God, not made; of the same essence as the Father . . . he became incarnate by the Holy Spirit and the virgin Mary and was made human."

Under the section about the Holy Spirit the Nicene Creed states "He proceeds from the Father and the Son." This sentence eventually led to the split between Christians in the east and Christians in the west, between what we know today as the Roman Catholic Church (the west) and the Eastern Orthodox Church. The split took place in 1054, with the Eastern church believing that the Holy Spirit proceeds only from the Father.

The third major creed is the Athanasian Creed, generally

thought to be written in the period between A.D. 381-428. It is seven or eight times as long as the Apostle's Creed and about five times as long as the Nicene Creed. The Athanasian Creed has been compared to a summary of Scripture.

All of these creeds insist on:

1. **The Trinity.** God is three separate and distinct persons: Father, Son, and Holy Spirit. A healthy church will cling to this doctrine as a bedrock truth.

2. **Jesus.** The Son of God is fully human *and* fully God. He was born of a virgin, lived a sinless life, and died voluntarily to pay the penalty for sin. By rising from the dead on the third day, He defeated once and for all the power of death. He alone did this; no one else shared in the work of redemption.

3. **Holy Spirit.** The Spirit of God works in the lives of men and women to teach us of Christ, to lead us to repentance, and to transform us into the likeness of Christ.

4. **The universal church.** The church is the entire body of Christ's followers; it is not a denomination or group.

5. **The Bible.** "All Scripture is God-breathed and is useful for teaching, rebuking, correcting and training in righteousness, so that the man of God may be thoroughly equipped for every good work" (2 Timothy 3:16-17). The Bible is the final authority on all matters of doctrine, superseding church traditions and the teachings of men.

6. **Salvation by grace through faith.** Faith, and faith alone, leads to salvation and eternal life.

When you find a Christ-centered church and ministry that proclaim the core teachings of Christianity, become a part of it.

Contribute your time, treasures, and talents to that little piece of the kingdom of God. Give your heart to sharing the good news of God's grace with others, and make sure that they know the difference between *Bad News Religion* and God's amazing grace.

FINDING A HEALTHY CHURCH—FREE FROM RELIGION

We need to reject legalism in all of its forms. We also need, as we have been given God's grace, to be part of his work on earth. As you look for a healthy, well-balanced church, here are some things to keep in mind:

- Look for a church where Christ is the center and focus of the preaching and where the Bible is the final authority. If that doesn't happen, move on down the road.
- If you visit a church and suspect some minimizing and diminishing of God's grace and the centrality of Jesus Christ, then question the pastor. Ask what his focus is. Always challenge performance-based religion. Examine the statements of faith and mission statements of the congregation and denomination. Be sure you read the complete statement of belief, not an abbreviated version. Find out what they really believe.
- If your church or religious group spends time and effort explaining a lot of stuff about the founder of the church or group, that's a huge red flag. If anyone other than God or the Bible is cited as a source of authority for behavior or doctrine, that's another red flag. Christianity is all about Jesus.
- Be on guard for a pastor or church that tells you that everyone else is wrong. Watch for enticing rhetoric, which claims that no one knows the "truth" except this group. If you hear talk about special anointings, inside revelation, and esoteric knowledge, head for the parking lot.

- Find out where your church or group stands on the historic Christian faith. A healthy church does not see itself or promote itself as outside of what Christ has done here on earth for almost 2,000 years, but as a part of it. A healthy, well-balanced church finds its identity in Jesus Christ and his body, the historic Christian faith. If a church finds its identity in some other way or in some other name, keep on looking, you haven't found a healthy church! If they talk about themselves as being a restoration of truth that no one has experienced since the New Testament, reach for your car keys or head for the bus stop.

- Consider the extent of authority. Red flags include authoritarian pastors who will not allow questions about their leadership or the direction of the church. While there is no one biblical model of church governance which will characterize authentic Christianity, absolute and dictatorial control in the hands of one person is a breeding ground of abuse and heresy. If you hear that the pastor or other leaders are exempt from accountability because they have a "spiritual covering," keep looking. You can be almost certain that you haven't found authentic Christianity.

- Absolute and dictatorial control in the hands of a church board that legislates and enforces religious legalism is just as bad as the same domination in the hands of one person. Authentic Christianity seems to function best with checks and balances, with all human leadership held accountable to standards, for the health and vitality of the entire congregation, denomination, and the body of Christ at large.

- Find out how they talk about and treat those who leave. If this is part of authentic Christianity, people will not be browbeaten and threatened if they decide to change their spiritual address from one healthy church to another.

- Look for a church that is not threatened by education or

academic credentials. If education is derided and science is characterized as evil, then the church has something to hide. Authentic Christianity is logical and coherent. It has nothing to hide and thrives on questions about all of its teachings.

- Sermons in a healthy church are centered in the Bible. The Bible is the source of the gospel, not shoe-horned as an after-thought into a feel-good lesson or experience.

- Look for Christ-centered substance, meaning, and relevance. Be suspicious of glitz, entertainment for its own sake, and an emphasis on emotional feeling.

- Beware of exotic manifestations, claims of unique prophetic insights, guarantees of health and wealth and healing, and revival crusades that seem to be more hype than reality.

- A healthy church will accept the basic, fundamental, and essential core doctrines of Christianity. Jude 3 tells us that the faith has been once and for all entrusted to the saints. Jesus said that the gates of hell would not prevail against his church. So we can look to the history of Christianity to find those teachings that have been examined, affirmed, and re-affirmed, as well as issues that have been redefined and reformed.

- Finally, and perhaps most importantly, listen and look for grace. You will hear lots of sermons about grace in a healthy church. You will even witness and enjoy some gracious behavior. You will see and hear Jesus, not religion. The health of a church is directly related to its emphasis and insistence on God's grace.

CHAPTER TWELVE —REVIEW AND RECAP

Burned Out. Many have given up on God because of the toxic teachings and practices of *Bad News Religion*. They are spiritually confused and often looking for answers in all the wrong places.

Grand Inquisitors. For the Grand Inquisitors of religion the issue is control. By God's grace we are offered freedom in Christ.

Don't give up! God will never give up on us—don't give up on him because someone did a less than adequate job representing him.

Comfortably incarcerated. Many people are comfortable in prison cells of *Bad News Religion,* and refuse the freedom that only Jesus can bring. The incarnation of Jesus is the answer to religious incarceration.

Finding a healthy church. If you are part of a church or group that teaches and practices *Bad News Religion,* look for a healthy Christ-centered church that emphasizes and insists on God's grace.

Red flags. As you prayerfully seek a healthy church, there are key indicators you can observe and questions you can ask that will help alert you to problems—and help identify a biblically-based, Christ-centered Church.

Conclusion: We Have a New Name

FEW BURDENS IN LIFE are as heavy as debt. Debts, whether physical or spiritual, can overwhelm us as we struggle to deal with the oppression of repayment and restitution. Thanks be to God, we have been saved from our spiritual debts by the cross of Christ! But salvation involves much more than the cancellation of our debts. Salvation essentially means "to be saved from a life-threatening situation." The Bible speaks of our salvation as being past, present, and future:

1. *We have been saved.* There was a definite time in history, the cross of Christ, when we were saved.

2. *We are being saved.* God justifies and sanctifies us, imputing to us the righteousness of Christ, seeing us as holy and calling us his saints. God works in us, empowering us to grow in his grace and knowledge, renewing us day by day. Our position and status with God right now is that we are saved.

3. *We will be saved.* We will experience the fullness of our salvation when we are resurrected, in God's kingdom of heaven, when we will be with him and enjoy his presence for eternity.

When we speak of salvation, it is imperative that we give God the glory. Salvation is a work of God alone. Salvation is not something humans *achieve;* it is something humans can only *receive,* by God's grace. Salvation is not a human enterprise. Humans do not participate in the work of salvation in any way.

Salvation is accomplished and applied by God. Salvation is *of* the Lord and *from* the Lord. Salvation is the rescue that our Savior alone wins for us, and we can claim no credit whatsoever.

The cross of Christ and his resurrection form the foundation of all we believe and the beginning of our new life in Christ. There are many theological and biblical terms that describe our salvation. Here are a few:

- *Adoption:* God confers upon us his special favor, grace, and all the benefits of being his very children. He makes us heirs of his kingdom.
- *Atonement:* Jesus Christ, as the Lamb of God, took our place. He substituted for us, bearing the penalty and debt of our sin. Jesus atoned for our sins on the cross once and for all.
- *Forgiveness:* God pardoned our wrongdoing. He eliminated our debt, the penalty of our sin. His forgiveness empowers us to do the same for others.
- *Justification:* God declares us righteous because of the finished work of Christ.
- *Reconciliation:* God removed the barrier of sin and reconciled us to himself in Christ.
- *Redemption:* Jesus Christ purchased us with his blood, paid the penalty for our sins, bought us out of slavery, and gave us freedom in him.
- *Regeneration:* God gives us new life in Christ.
- *Sanctification:* God pronounces us holy and by the Holy Spirit works in us to conform us to Christ. Sanctification is the act of God that brings our moral condition into conformity with the legal status established in justification.

Jesus Christ really did pay a debt he didn't owe because we owe a debt we cannot pay. It's the plain truth—not a trite cliché. When God forgives us, our debt is paid—in full. We have no debts or liabilities. But neither do we have any assets. The act of justification and sanctification means that God imputes the righteousness of Jesus Christ to us. He makes a huge deposit of grace in our spiritual bank account. He gives us the riches of his grace. We become new men and women. We are God's very own children.

I believe that every church should have a department or office of reformation. Every church should have reformers who work to challenge sacred cows that in turn become golden calves that *Bad News Religion* uses to advance its own purposes, instead of the kingdom of God. Some churches, especially Lutherans, could call it the Martin Luther endowed chair of reformation and repentance.

Don't Exchange the Precious Gift of God's Grace For *Bad News Religion!*

In the stage version of *Man of La Mancha* (based on Cervantes' novel, *Don Quixote De La Mancha*), the hero Don Quixote meets a woman named Aldonza in a little town in Spain. She is a harlot at night, while during the day she is a waitress.

Don Quixote falls in love with Aldonza, telling her that he believes that one day he will be a knight, and of course every knight must have a lady. He tells Aldonza that he has decided that she will be his lady.

Don Quixote declares his love for Aldonza, refusing to see her as the fallen woman she is but as what she can become—his lady. "Sweet lady...fair virgin, I dare not gaze upon thy countenance lest I be blinded by beauty. I will give you a name, a new name, Dulcinea. I have sought thee, sung thee, dreamed thee, and the world shall know thy glory, Dulcinea!"

Aldonza is a hardened veteran of the real world, where men use and abuse her. She responds, "My name is Aldonza. Men make passes at me."

But Don Quixote is undaunted. Each time he sees her he says, "Dulcinea, my lady. You are my lady." She responds to his kindness by spitting on the ground and bargaining for more money with a potential customer.

With this background the play takes a sudden turn. The curtain rises to an empty stage. Suddenly Aldonza runs across the stage bare footed, wet with sweat, straw clinging to her clothing that has been ripped and torn away from her. She has been raped.

> God has given you and me a new name. We are regenerated. We are his children.

She's weeping, almost hysterical. Suddenly the man of La Mancha appears and runs to her side. "Oh, my lady," he says with love and compassion. But she can't accept his grace. She screams at him, "O my God, don't call me your lady. Look at me, can't you see me for what I really am? I was born in a ditch, by a mother who left me there, naked, cold and too hungry to cry. I never blamed her. I'm sure she left hoping I would have the good sense to die. Look at me. I'm no lady. I'm only a kitchen slut oozing with sweat, a horror that men use and forget. Don't call me a lady. I am nothing. Nothing at all." And she runs off the stage.

Don Quixote, the man of La Mancha is unmoved. He stares at her as she runs away and insists, "But you are my lady, you are my lady." Then the curtain drops.

When the curtain rises for the next act, Don Quixote is on his deathbed. The dreamer of impossible dreams is dying. He is despised and rejected by others. He is a man of sorrows, acquainted with grief.

A beautiful woman comes to his deathbed, dressed in a mantilla made of black lace that covers her head and shoulders and veils her face. She kneels and prays, then looks at him and says, "My Lord..."

Quixote does not recognize her and asks, "Who are you?"

She responds, "My Lord, don't you remember? Try to remember. You sang a song, remember?

> To dream the impossible dream,
> To fight the unbeatable foe,
> To bear with unbearable sorrow,
> To run where the brave dare not go.
> This is my quest, to follow that star,
> No matter how hopeless, no matter how far.
> And I know, if I'll only be true to this glorious quest
> That my heart will lie peaceful and calm
> When I'm laid to my rest.
> And the world will be better for this,
> That one man, scorned and covered with scars,
> Still strove, with his last ounce of courage
> To reach the unreachable stars!

She is crying. "Don't you remember my Lord?" She draws her mantilla back and she says, "You gave me a new name. You called me Dulcinea." With his last human effort the man of La Mancha tries to rise out of his bed, but cannot, and falling back to die, with his last words he says, "My lady."

Aldonza faces the audience and pronounces, "My name is Dulcinea."

God has given you and me a new name. We are *regenerated*. We are his children, spiritually re-born and *adopted,* heirs of his kingdom. The blood of Christ has *atoned* for our sin. We are *forgiven, redeemed,* and *reconciled.* God has justified and sanctified us, making us righteous and holy in his sight. God has saved us, is saving us and will save us, by Christ alone, by faith alone, and by grace alone.

This is the love of God that was poured out for us on the cross, and this is the victory over sin and death that was won at the resurrection of our Lord. Jesus is both Savior and Lord. And you, by God's matchless, amazing, and supreme grace, are a child of God.

God will never let you go, never give up on you, or never forsake you. He has either already saved you by his grace, or his hand is stretched out welcoming you into the world of his grace. Whatever you do, don't give away or surrender the precious gift of God's grace to anyone. You have a new name; don't trade it for *Bad News Religion.*

ABOUT THE AUTHOR

GREG ALBRECHT is Executive Director of Plain Truth Ministries (PTM), host of *Plain Truth* radio and editor-in-chief of *Plain Truth* magazine.

His journey to Christ has taken him through what he calls *40 Miles of Bad Road* of religion, cultic teachings, and legalism. His ministry is dedicated to exposing and explaining unbiblical and cultic teachings that masquerade as authentic Christianity, attempting to turn it into *Bad News Religion.*

Through his ministry Greg insists that authentic Christianity is based on God's amazing grace, and often asks whether the gospel is getting lost in religion. He believes religious legalism is doing its best to obliterate God's amazing grace. For more information about the ongoing ministry of PTM visit www.ptm.org.

In addition to hosting *Plain Truth* radio, Greg has also been a guest on many Christian radio and television programs. Greg lives in California with his wife Karen, and is a much-traveled speaker, addressing churches and conferences around the world. Greg and Karen are proud parents of two married children and their families.